LEGENDARY BOXERS
OF THE GOLDEN AGE

MIKE DALY,

Bangor, Me.

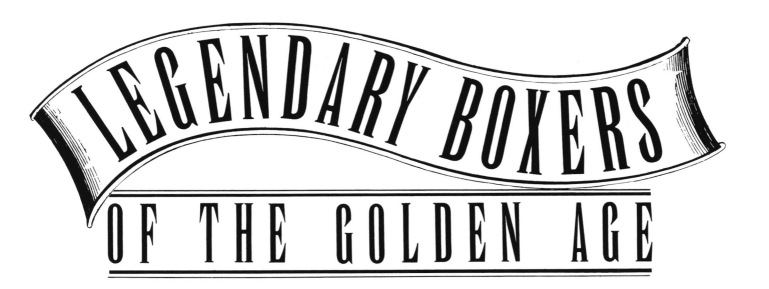

LEGENDARY BOXERS
OF THE GOLDEN AGE

of

ENGLAND,

AMERICA,

AUSTRALIA

WITH BIOGRAPHICAL SKETCHES AND AUTHENTIC RECORDS OF
THEIR VICTORIES AND DEFEATS

EMBRACING

THE MEN OF NOTE OF ALL NATIONS CONNECTED
WITH THE PUGILISTIC ARENA

BY

BILLY EDWARDS

Ex-Champion Light Weight

IN HOC SIGNO VINCES

southwater

This edition is published by Southwater,
an imprint of Anness Publishing Ltd,
Blaby Road, Wigston, Leicestershire LE18 4SE

info@anness.com

www.southwaterbooks.com;
www.annesspublishing.com

If you like the images in this book and would like to investigate using them for
publishing, promotions or advertising, please visit our website
www.practicalpictures.com for more information.

This edition © Anness Publishing Ltd 2013

A CIP catalogue record for this book is available from the British Library.

Hand-marbled paper on jacket and cover
© Mitchell and Malik Ltd.

CONTENTS

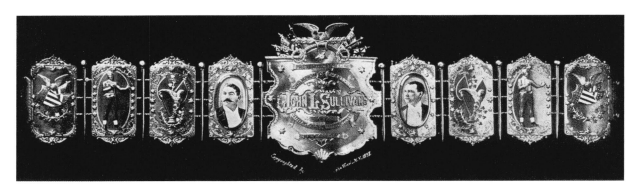

THE JOHN L. SULLIVAN DIAMOND BELT.

INTRODUCTION

THE Author believes that in presenting this volume to the public, he is filling a long-felt want, particularly in the great sporting world. Of recent years the interest taken in the noble art of self-defense has been almost universal. The cultivation in our colleges and other institutions of learning of athletic exercise, and the great interest taken by all classes of people in physical culture, would seem to indicate that this is the golden era of *muscular development*, and the establishment of a perfect manhood and womanhood.

"THE PUGILISTIC PORTRAIT GALLERY" has been prepared in the most careful manner, under my personal supervision. Every fact has been verified by exhaustive research and careful compilation of official data. Every important event in the fistic arena, from the first ring encounter down to the great battles of the present day, both in this country and abroad, is given a place. The biographical matter is historically correct, and the accompanying illustrations are taken from authentic photographs or sketches made from life.

In faithfully describing a ring battle, the observations of one witness — no matter how careful and minute — are insufficient. To properly write the history of such an encounter, the chronicler must draw impartially from a variety of sources. Each witness will be more or less prejudiced, and will let his bias color his account. The careful historian must conscientiously compare these several reports, sift out that which is immaterial and incorrect, and preserve only such details as a majority of the witnesses agree upon. In every instance, in describing latter day battles, this has been done.

Newspaper accounts of a fistic combat are full of in-accuracies which slip in because of the hurried manner in which they have to be written. The accounts in this book are composite compilations from the personal experiences of those best competent to describe the events – the principals, seconds, timekeepers, backers, referee, &c. – and have been carefully edited and are concisely presented.

The book will be found unexcelled as an accurate work of reference, for not a fact has been distorted nor a line set down in malice.

Truly yours,

BILLY EDWARDS,
(Ex-Light Weight Champion of the World.)

THE GALLERY

OF PUGILISTS

BILLY EDWARDS,

EX-LIGHT WEIGHT CHAMPION OF THE WORLD.

BILLY EDWARDS was born December 21, 1844, in Birmingham, Warwickshire, England. His fighting weight was one hundred and twenty-six pounds, his height is five feet, five inches.

His record is as follows:—Beat Sam Colyer, August 24, 1868, forty-seven rounds, one hour and fourteen minutes, $1,000 (£200) a side; Sam Colyer, March 2, 1870, forty rounds, forty-five minutes, $1,000 (£200). Draw with Tim Collins, May 25, 1871, ninety-five rounds, two hours fifteen minutes, $1,000 (£200). Beaten by Arthur Chambers, September 4, 1872, twenty-six rounds, one hour thirty-five minutes, $1,000 (£200); lost by an alleged foul. Beat William Fauceth, March 13, 1873, fifty-five rounds, one hour fifty-five minutes, $500 (£100); Sam Colyer, August 8, 1874, ten rounds, twenty-four minutes, $1,000 (£200).

He was presented with the Light Weight Championship of the World Belt, December 24, 1874, in New York City.

This portrait was kindly loaned the Pugilistic Publishing Company by Arthur Chambers. It was taken when Billy Edwards was in his prime, and is the only one in existence.

BILLY EDWARDS,

Ex-Light Weight Champion of the World.

JAMES JOHN CORBETT,

CHAMPION OF THE WORLD.

HE pugilistic history of the present World's champion, JAMES JOHN CORBETT, has been a short one, but it has been full of honor. He first saw the light of day on September 1, 1866, in San Francisco, California, and was, therefore, just twenty-six years old when he met John Lawrence Sullivan for the championship of America. His parents were Irish, and they gave their son a good education in the public schools of San Francisco, and at the Catholic College of the Sacred Heart. In these days he was noted as a frank, brave, quick-tempered boy, or as one of his contemporaries put it: "A good fellow to have for a friend, but an enemy to be dreaded." He used to whip boys several years older than himself, and was unexcelled in all athletic sports.

After leaving the College he was employed in the Bank of Nevada, in a minor position, later being promoted to a clerkship in that rich institution. He was well liked by his fellow clerks and by the officials, and but for his fondness for the "manly art," might have been content to win moderate success in this quiet and respectable sphere in life.

His first instruction in boxing was received from Prof. Walter Watkins, of the Olympic Athletic Club. In 1884, when but eighteen years of age, he made his first appearance in a professional way, his opponent being Dave Eisemann, now a well-known pool seller. Two rounds sufficed to settle Mr. Eisemann. James C. Dailey was his next opponent, and he got enough in four rounds. "Buffalo" Costello, who was considered a wonderful fighter at the time, got the worst of a three-round contest with the rising young pugilist, and he subsequently defeated Duncan McDonald, of Butte, Montana, in four rounds.

Corbett was then engaged to teach boxing in the Olympic Club, and before the year closed had met and defeated Joe Choynski three times, once in one round, once in two and once in four rounds, and proved equally victorious in his contests with other noted fighters. His first opponent, after the easy victory over Choynski, was Jack Burke, the "Irish Lad," who had successfully stood up against such knights of the ring as Sullivan, Slavin, Mitchell and Dempsey. It was an eight-round affair, and was declared a draw. Frank Smith succumbed to Corbett in three rounds, and then came Mike Brennan, the "Port Costa Giant." He had fought Joe McAuliffe forty rounds, but Corbett easily disposed of him in four rounds. Not satisfied to rest upon his laurels, the Pacific Slope boy followed this fight with others, defeating George Atkinson, in two rounds, and Frank Glover, of Chicago, in two.

In December, of 1884, he met Joe Choynski on a barge in the Sacramento River, and again defeated him in a hard-fought battle of twenty-seven rounds, during which he broke his hand. He got decidedly the best of it with Prof. William Miller, in a three-round contest, fought a five-round

JAMES JOHN CORBETT,
Champion of the World.

battle with Choynski, which came to an end because of police interference, and easily got the decision in a four-round meet for points, with Joe McAuliffe. He still continued as teacher in the Olympic Club, and had an easily won contest with Dave Campbell, of Portland, Oregon.

On February 17, 1890, Corbett met Jake Kilrain, of Baltimore, in a six-round glove contest, before the Southern Athletic Club, of New Orleans, for a purse of $3,500, and was declared the winner. He then went North on a sparring tour, and on April 14, 1890, at the Fifth Avenue Casino, Brooklyn, N. Y., defeated Dominick F. McCaffrey, in a sharp and hotly contested battle, during the third round.

Returning to San Francisco, Corbett issued, in the summer of 1890, a challenge to fight any man in the world for $5,000 a side, and on the night of May 21–22, 1891, Peter Jackson, the negro pugilist, met him before the California Athletic Club, for a purse of $10,000. At the close of the sixty-first round both men were physically unable to continue the battle, and the referee decided that it was a draw.

Corbett's first great victory was when he defeated John L. Sullivan, of Boston, before the Olympic Club, of New Orleans, for a stake of $20,000, and a purse of $25,000, thereby securing the title of Champion of the World. The battle was fought on the night of September 7, 1892, and was finished in the twenty-first round. He was soon thereafter challenged by Charlie Mitchell, champion of England, and on January 25, 1894, before the Duval Athletic Club, of Jacksonville, Florida, for a purse of $20,000 and a stake of $10,000, met and defeated Mitchell in a sharply contested battle, lasting but three rounds, thereby securing his present title, champion of the World.

The champion is 6 feet, 1½ inches in height, in his stockings, and weighs about 190 pounds. He is quick and cat-like in his movements, and a hard hitter, having knocked out no less than twenty-five men, some of them outweighing him forty pounds. Under the management of William A. Brady, he has been very successful as a theatrical star, appearing as "Jack Rawdon," in the drama "Gentleman Jack," written specially for him, in which, in March, 1894, he began a highly profitable engagement at the Old Drury Lane Theatre, London, England. He has been challenged by his old opponent, Peter Jackson, and it is probable that the two men will soon meet. The champion is a married man and very domestic in his habits. He is the first and only American pugilist who ever visited England without being challenged.

"GENTLEMAN JIM."

THE CORBETT-MITCHELL FIGHT.

AFTER long and vexatious delays, which were of such a nature that the great sporting world began to believe that the two men would never come together, Corbett and Charley Mitchell, Champion of England, met at last, on January 25, 1894, before the Duval Athletic Club, of Jacksonville, Florida, for a purse of $20,000, a stake of $10,000, and the championship of the World.

The proposed meeting had been vigorously opposed by the then Governor of the State of Florida, Mitchell, and he was backed by a very respectable majority of the citizens. He declared that the fight should never take place, and called out the military to enforce his authority. He was prevented from going to extreme measures by a decision of the Supreme Court, which declared that no law would be violated by the pugilists in the settlement of the question of the championship.

There was a feeling of great bitterness between the two men, and it was known that it would be a battle for blood. To the surprise of many the contest was of only three rounds duration. In the first round Mitchell appeared to have the best of the fight, and his partizans went wild.

"Where is your Gentleman Jim, now?" came in a rollicking chorus from the ring side. "He carries his nerve in his shoes!"

Corbett had got the measure of his man, however, and in the second round his longer reach and superior strength began to tell. Mitchell was knocked down, but managed to get upon his feet and retreated before his enemy until the gong sounded. The third round was of short duration. Corbett pursued his man with relentless fury, raining blow after blow upon his face and body. A terrific blow in the jaw sent Mitchell to the floor like a slaughtered ox. He managed to get upon his feet, but Corbett rushed upon him and another terrible face blow ended the fight.

Both men were subsequently arrested by the authorities, and gave bail for their appearance. When their cases came to trial they were discharged, there being no law on the statute books of the State to punish them. John Kelly, of New York, was the referee. Prof. John Donaldson, Billy Delaney, Jack Dempsey and John McVey, were Corbett's seconds, while Mitchell was looked after by Pony Moore, Tom Allen and Steve O'Donnell. Ted Foley was Corbett's timekeeper, while Mitchell's interests were attended to by Bat Masterson. The celebrated jockey, Snapper Garrison, was the Club's timekeeper.

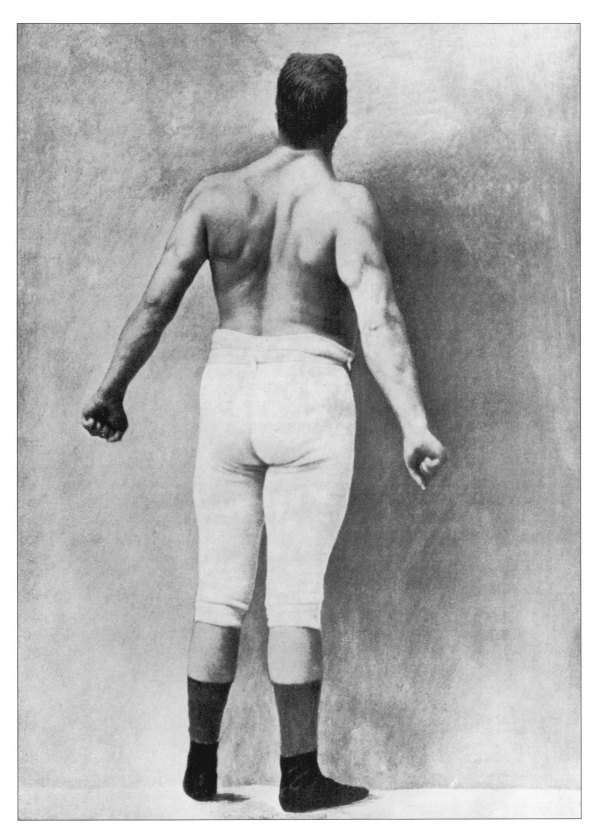

CHARLIE MITCHELL,
Champion of England.

THE CORBETT-SULLIVAN FIGHT.

IN the arena of the Olympic Club, New Orleans, La., September 7, 1892, John L. Sullivan met his Waterloo, being knocked out by Corbett in the twenty-first round. The fight was for the largest sum ever known, a purse of $25,000, and a side bet of $10,000. Seven thousand people witnessed this great fistic battle, and the excitement and enthusiasm reached fever heat.

In this limited space it would be impossible to describe the fight by rounds.

It was a triumph of youth, agility and skill over advancing years, over-confidence and strength. It was a victory of mind over matter.

Sullivan was seconded by Charles Johnson and Jack McAuliffe, with Frank Moran as timekeeper. The men who stood behind Corbett were Prof. John Donaldson and Billy Delaney. Bat Masterson was his timekeeper and Philip Dwyer, the turfman, was final stakeholder. Promptly at 9 o'clock the two principals shook hands, and, after a moment's parleying regarding the rules, prepared for hostilities. The battle began at 9.05 o'clock.

For the first round Corbett adopted dodging tactics, and the crowd yelled at him. After this round, and in the rounds which followed, he took the initiative and forced the fighting. As the battle proceeded it was seen that Sullivan was being beaten, and a great feeling of sympathy went up for the man who had held the championship so long.

He struggled manfully to rush down his young opponent, but Corbett's telling blows dazed and bewildered him, and when time was called for the twenty-first round, the Californian rushed in and planted blow after blow on Sullivan's face and neck. The latter backed away, trying to save himself; but Corbett was close upon him, and when, bleeding and exhausted, with glassy eyes and trembling limbs, he lowered his guard from sheer exhaustion, the young Californian shot his right across the champion's jaw, and he fell like an ox.

When finally he arose, bruised and bleeding, and staggering to the ropes, moved his battered and swollen lips, there issued these words, in a tone hoarse with chagrin and weakness:

"It's the old, old story. I am like the pitcher that went to the well once too often." His voice broke, and gulping down a sob, he continued: "I can only say that I am glad that I have been beaten by an American."

JOHN L. SULLIVAN,
Ex-Champion of the World.

THE CORBETT-JACKSON DRAW.

IN the summer of 1890, after his return to California from a sparring tour through the Eastern, Middle and Middle Western States, Corbett issued a challenge to fight any man in the world for $5,000 a side, and on the night of May 21–22, 1891, Peter Jackson, the negro pugilist, met him in San Francisco for a purse of $10,000, $1500 to go to the loser, offered by the California Athletic Club.

The majority of San Francisco sporting men seemed to think that Corbett had made a mistake in tackling the sable Australian, and the betting was largely in Jackson's favor. When they entered the ring Corbett weighed 168 pounds and Jackson 204. The battle was a long and fierce one, but at the close of the sixty-first round, both men were physically unable to continue the fight, and the referee decided that it was "no contest," and each pugilist received $2,500, with the privilege of fighting again for $7,500. It had lasted four hours and three minutes, and was one of the most stubborn fights in the history of the prize ring.

It was at the close of this fight that Corbett made a tour of the United States and challenged John L. Sullivan to fight for $10,000 a side.

Jackson is the champion of Australia and the colored champion of the world. It is likely that in the near future he will contest with Corbett for the title without color bar. He was born in the West Indies in 1861, but the greater portion of his life has been spent in Australia. He is a giant in stature, standing six feet one and one-half inches in height, and in training weighs 205 pounds. He became known as a pugilist in 1883, when he fought his first battle at Larry Foley's Hall, Sydney, N. S. W.

Since he began to fight he has met at least fifteen men, the very cream of Australian pugilism. In 1888 he arrived at San Francisco, California, since which time he has met and defeated the following men, outside of Champion Corbett, with whom he fought a draw: George Godfrey, the colored champion of America, for a purse of $2,000, at the California Athletic Club, August 24, 1888; Joe McAuliffe, at the same place, for a purse of $3,000, December 29, 1888; Patsey Cardiff, at the rooms of the California Club, for a purse of $3,000, April 26, 1889; Jem Smith, the English champion, at the rooms of the Pelican Club, London, England, for a purse of $5,000, $4,000 to go to the winner and $1,000 to the loser, November 11, 1889; Paddy Slavin, at the rooms of the Pelican Club, London, England, for a purse of $12,500, May 30, 1892.

Under the management of Parson Davies, of Chicago, Jackson has toured through this country, during the past season, appearing as *Uncle Tom*, in Harriet Beecher Stowe's popular play, "Uncle Tom's Cabin."

PETER JACKSON,
Champion of Australia.

THE CORBETT-CHOYNSKI FIGHTS.

IN the days when Corbett was first beginning to attract attention as a rising young pugilist who had the making of a champion in him, one of the men who most persistently contested with him, and seemed always willing to stand in the way of his triumphant progress upward and onward, was Joe Choynski.

Within the space of a few months, in 1884–85, the two men met no less than three times. In the fall of 1884, at the rooms of the San Francisco Olympic Club, Corbett easily defeated Choynski in one round, but this did not satisfy the latter. Another match was arranged later, for a big side bet, and the two men met in a barn just over the county line. During the fifth round the police made a descent upon the place and the battle was postponed until a more auspicious day.

Just after the beginning of the new year, and little more than a week from the last meeting, the two men faced each other again on the deck of a barge in the middle of the Sacramento River. On this occasion Choynski had behind him the then champion middle-weight, Jack Dempsey.

Choynski wore gloves heavily ribbed, that would cut a man if landed fairly and squarely. Corbett's gloves were of the ordinary driving variety, minus the ribs. More money was wagered on this event than on any that had ever taken place in California, and the betting was even. It was a bloody battle of twenty-seven rounds. Choynski made a game fight, but he was manifestly outclassed, and, although Corbett broke one of his hands early in the fight. and seriously hurt the other, he defeated his opponent.

After this evidence of pugilistic prowess, Corbett returned to his old position of teacher of boxing in the Olympic Club, and was hailed by its members, who fairly idolized him, as the coming champion. He was only nineteen years of age, and the world was all before him.

Joe Choynski is one of the cleverest of the heavy weights. Besides meeting Corbett he has stood up before nearly every pugilist of prominence in the country.

He went to Australia in 1891, and on May 25th of that year, at Melbourne, defeated Mick Dooley for a purse, in two rounds, lasting four minutes and eleven seconds. Returning to America he met George Godfrey, the colored heavy weight, at West Brighton Beach, Coney Island, October 31st, 1892, for a purse of $5,000, and defeated him in fifteen rounds, lasting fifty-nine minutes.

Joe Choynski's last contest was with Bob Fitzsimmons, on June 18th, 1894, at the Boston Theatre, Boston, Mass. The men were to spar eight rounds, and but for Choynski's hot-headedness he might have won. The police stopped the contest in the fifth round, and referee Bill Daly declared it a draw.

JOE CHOYNSKI,
San Francisco, Cal.

THE CORBETT-McCAFFREY GLOVE CONTEST.

AFTER his defeat of Jake Kilrain in a six-round go for points at New Orleans, Corbett went North on a sparring tour. On the night of April 14, 1890, at the Fifth Avenue Casino, Brooklyn, N. Y., he was tendered a benefit, on which occasion he had a three-round contest with Dominick F. McCaffrey. He made game of the Eastern man, outgeneraling him at every point.

The terms were three rounds for scientific points. This did not altogether please the 2,500 spectators, who wanted to see a knock-out. Several Californians were in the audience. In the first two rounds the sparring was light, but in the third and last round Corbett received hearty applause, when he demonstrated how easy it was for him to do as he pleased with McCaffrey.

Steve O'Donnell, the referee, had no occasion for hesitation in giving Corbett the decision. Johnny Reagan was timekeeper.

McCaffrey is a native of Pittsburg, Pa., and received a good education in the public schools. It was the intention of his parents to make him a Catholic priest, but his fondness for athletics turned the bent of his mind naturally toward those sports, and when he was only a lad of fourteen he was known in the "Smoky City" as a very clever boxer.

In 1883 McCaffrey went to Philadelphia, and appeared at several of the sporting resorts in contests with gloves. He was willing to meet any one, and a match was arranged between him and the English champion, Charlie Mitchell, which came off at Madison Square Garden, New York City, October 13, 1884. Four rounds were fought, McCaffrey winning. On August 29, 1885, he met John L. Sullivan, at Cincinnati, Ohio, in a six-round glove contest, in which Sullivan got the decision. He afterwards met and defeated "Sparrow" Golden, and was in turn defeated by Jack Dempsey, in a ten-round glove fight, at Jersey City, New Jersey, January 31, 1888.

With the exception of his contest with Corbett, McCaffrey has but seldom made a public appearance as a boxer since his defeat by Dempsey. He is the boxing teacher of the Manhattan Athletic Club, New York City, and is a man of quiet, domestic tastes.

DOMINICK McCAFFREY,

Pittsburgh, Pa.

THE CORBETT-BURKE DRAW.

IN 1887, when he was only a boy, but with a reputation that was constantly growing as a courageous and scientific fighter, Corbett was matched to fight Jack Burke, the "Irish Lad." He was at this time boxing teacher in the San Francisco Olympic Club, and had established for himself quite a record as a gamey pugilist, but the wise ones shook their heads when the contest with Burke was announced.

The "Irish Lad" was a fighter of experience and reputation. He had successfully stood against such giants of the ring as John L. Sullivan, Frank P. Slavin, Charley Mitchell and Jack Dempsey. This Pacific Slope stripling, it was thought, would have no show with such a hardened veteran.

It was, perhaps, these adverse criticisms, and a lack of confidence in his own superb abilities, born of inexperience, that made Corbett extraordinarily cautious and careful. The contest lasted eight rounds, and was declared a draw; but the opinion was general among those who witnessed the fight, that had Corbett been less careful he could easily have whipped his man.

On March 2, 1885, Jack Burke beat Alf Greenfield in a five-round contest with gloves, at Chicago, Illinois, and on March 23, again met him and fought a draw. Previous to this, on October 21, 1884, he had fought a draw with Charley Mitchell, at New York. He met John L. Sullivan on June 13, 1885, at Chicago, Illinois, in a five-round contest, and was beaten. On the 29th of the same month he again fought a draw with Charley Mitchell at Chicago.

On November 23, 1885, he was pitted against Mike Cleary, in a glove contest at San Francisco, California. After fighting nine rounds the police interfered and the contest was declared a draw. On the 28th of the following December, the two again met at Chicago, Illinois, and Burke was declared the winner in three rounds. In 1889 Burke went to Australia, and on February 4th of that year was bested by Paddy Slavin in a glove contest.

JACK BURKE,

The Irish Lad.

JOHN LAWRENCE SULLIVAN,

THE CHAMPION OF CHAMPIONS.

OHN LAWRENCE SULLIVAN, who has been very justly termed the "Champion of Champions," he having met and defeated more first-class men than any other pugilist, was born in Boston, Massachusetts, October 15, 1858, of Irish parents, they having emigrated to Boston Highlands, from County Kerry, Ireland, a few years previous to his birth. He received an education in the public schools of his native city, and his early displayed fondness for athletics, first for baseball and later for boxing, won for him the title of "Strong Boy," he being, at the age of sixteen, invincible among his playmates as a fighter.

His boxing partner was Johnny Murphy, and two prominent "Hub" sporting men, Jim Keenan and Tom Earley, witnessed many bouts between the youngsters and predicted for the "Strong Boy" a brilliant future in the pugilistic arena.

In the Spring of 1880 he had two notable contests. At the Masonic Hall, Boston, Mass., he bested Joe Goss, the ex-champion, in three minutes, and in seven minutes, in New York City, defeated George Rooke. Keenan and Earley saw these bouts, and it was through their influence that a glove fight was arranged between the future champion and Professor John Donaldson, which came off at Cincinnati, Ohio, December 14, 1880. The fight lasted ten rounds, and was won by Sullivan in twenty-one minutes, he being awarded the $500 purse.

Those who witnessed the fight hailed the "Strong Boy" as the coming champion, and an unsuccessful effort was made by Richard K. Fox, of the *Police Gazette*, to bring about a match between him and Paddy Ryan.

Pending the signing of articles of agreement, Sullivan had a benefit at Harry Hill's, the date being March 31, 1881. He met the veteran Steve Taylor, and although the latter was defeated in three minutes, Sullivan determined to get a little more practical experience before meeting Ryan, and the *Police Gazette* negotiations for a fight between the two men fell through. On May 16, 1881, Sullivan met John Flood, of New York. The fight took place on a barge, anchored opposite Yonkers, on the Hudson River, and resulted in a victory for Sullivan in eight rounds, lasting sixteen minutes.

After this contest Sullivan had many successful bouts of four rounds' duration, and was encouraged to make a match with Ryan, who was the then champion of America. The fight was for $2,500 a side and the championship of America, and was fought February 7, 1882, at Mississippi City, Mississippi. It resulted in a victory for Sullivan in nine rounds, lasting eleven minutes.

At a benefit given to the champion at Washington Park, New York City, July 4, 1882, he was faced by Jim Elliott, who lasted but three rounds, fought in seven minutes and twenty seconds. On the seventeenth of the same month, at Madison Square Garden, Sullivan undertook to knock Joe Collins, better known as "Tug Wilson," the English pugilist, out of time in four rounds of three minutes each. He failed to accomplish the task. Subsequently the champion toured the country at the head of an athletic combination, meeting all comers.

From this time on, down to his final battle with Corbett, at New Orleans, Sullivan fought many battles. On May 14, 1883, at Madison Square Garden, New York City, he boxed Charley Mitchell, with medium-sized gloves, he to receive 60 per cent. of the admission receipts, and Mitchell the balance. The fight lasted three rounds, the police interfering. Sullivan had much the best of it. On August 6th, the same year, he met Herbert A. Slade, the "Maori," at Madison Square

JOHN L. SULLIVAN,

"Champion of Champions."

Garden, in a glove contest of four three-minute rounds. Slade gave up at the expiration of the third round.

In September, 1883, the champion started on a nine months' sparring tour of the United States and Territories, under the management of Al. Smith, who offered $1,000 to any man who would stand before Sullivan for four rounds. About fifty men in all tried to win the reward, but failed, all being knocked out in a few minutes, among whom were Captain Dalton, in eight minutes; Burns, the "Michigan Giant," in one minute and thirty seconds; Jack Stewart in thirty seconds, and Fred. Robinson, of Butte City, Montana, in four minutes.

On March 6th, 1884, at San Francisco, California, Sullivan had a glove fight with G. M. Robinson, four rounds, Queensbury rules, gate money division, and won an easy victory, Robinson going down sixty-eight times, to avoid punishment. On April 10, 1884, at Galveston, Texas, he defeated Alexander Marx, in one round; time one minute, fifty-five seconds. At Hot Springs, Arkansas, April 29, 1884, he knocked out Dan Henry in one round, time two minutes; and on May 1, 1884, in the short period of two seconds, he did a like service for William Fleming, at the Exposition Building, Memphis, Tennessee. The next day, at Nashville, Tennessee, he met and defeated Enos Phillips in four rounds; time seven minutes.

On November 17th, of the same year, he had a glove contest with Prof. J. M. Laflin, at the Madison Square Garden, New York City, of four rounds, for the gate money, and won easily in the third round; time seven minutes. One week later, on the seventeenth, he faced Alf. Greenfield, in the same arena, for the same stake. Two rounds, lasting six minutes, fifteen seconds, were fought, when the police interfered. Both principals were arrested and indicted for violating the law against prize fighting, but were acquitted December 17th. On January 12, 1885, at Boston, Massachusetts, in the New England Institute Building, Sullivan again met Greenfield, and in a four round contest, lasting twelve minutes, bested him. On January 19th he had a contest lasting thirty seconds, with Paddy Ryan, at Madison Square Garden. The police interfering, it was declared a draw.

At Driving Park, Chicago, Illinois, on June 13th, Sullivan had a five-round glove contest with Jack Burke, besting him; time fifteen minutes, and on August 29th, at Cincinnati, Ohio, he bested Dominick F. McCaffrey in a six-round contest. In 1886, on September 25, he met Frank Herald, at Pittsburg, Pa., in a glove contest, but the police stopped it in the second round, and on November 13th, at San Francisco, California, he knocked Paddy Ryan out in the third round of a glove contest.

Patsy Cardiff faced the champion at Minneapolis, Minnesota, on January 18, 1887, and although Sullivan broke the radius of his right arm early in the fight, he bested his opponent. On May 17th, Jake Kilrain challenged Sullivan to fight for $5,000 a side up, and the championship. The challenge was not accepted and Sullivan forfeited the title.

Sullivan sailed for Europe on October 17th, and upon his arrival in England boxed with Jack Ashton, appearing before the Prince of Wales on December 9th. On March 10, 1888, he and Charley Mitchell fought for $5,000, at Apremont, France. The fight lasted three hours and eleven minutes, and was declared a draw. Returning to this country, Sullivan challenged Jake Kilrain to fight for the championship of the world and $20,000, on December 7th.

Sullivan and Kilrain met July 8, 1889, at Richburg, Mississippi, and after seventy-five rounds, lasting two hours, sixteen minutes and twenty-three seconds, had been fought, Sullivan was declared the winner. In the arena of the Olympic Club, at New Orleans, La., September 7, 1892, Sullivan lost the championship to James J. Corbett, in a fight of twenty-one rounds, lasting one hour and twenty-three minutes.

Sullivan made his appearance on the theatrical stage on September 1, 1890, for the first time in a speaking part, personating *James Daly*, in "Honest Hands and Willing Hearts," at Niblo's Garden, New York City. Meeting with good success he concluded to adopt the stage as his profession. He is now starring through the country in a play of his own, which has been received with marked favor by theatre-goers.

JOHN LAWRENCE SULLIVAN,

"Champion of Champions."

THE SULLIVAN-RYAN FIGHTS.

ON February 7, 1882, a tremendous crowd assembled at Mississippi City, Mississippi, to witness the great battle for a purse of $5,000 and the championship of America, between John L. Sullivan and Patrick Ryan, the "Troy Terror."

The colors of the two pugilists were elaborate and costly. Ryan's were a white silk handkerchief, with red, white and blue border, representing the national colors. The central figure was an eagle standing on an azure globe, spangled. The inscription read : "Paddy Ryan, Champion of America." On the scroll held by the eagle were the words : "Police Gazette, New York, 1881." In the four corners were the figures and the words following :—A harp of Erin, a sun-burst, an American shield, an excelsior.

Sullivan's colors were a silk handkerchief with a green border, with Irish and Confederate flags in the corners. The figure occupied the centre, with this inscription underneath : "May the best man win." The ring was pitched on the lawn of Barnes' Hotel, and was admirably fitted for the purpose.

At 11.47 o'clock, A. M., Sullivan shied his helmet-shaped hat into the ring. He was dressed in his fighting shoes, green stockings, white flannel fighting breeches with green stripe and undershirt. At 12.02 Ryan entered the ring in a suit of white drawers and undershirt, flesh-colored stockings and fighting shoes.

Ryan won the toss for corners and placed his opponent facing the sun, he going to the southwest and Sullivan to the northeast. Harry Hill was final stakeholder. Jack Hardy, of Vicksburg, and Alexander Brewster, of New Orleans, were selected as referees. Arthur Chambers was the umpire for Sullivan, James Shannon for Ryan. Sullivan's seconds were Billy Madden and Joe Goss. Ryan was looked after by Tom Kelly, of St. Louis, Mo., and Johnny Roche, of New York. Sullivan weighed 193 pounds and Ryan 195. At the ring-side Ryan bet Sullivan $1,000 on the result of the fight, the stake being placed in the hands of Harry Hill. At 12.56 the fight began.

From the first it was seen that Sullivan was the better man of the two, but Ryan contested the honors with him gamely, and made a courageous fight. In the ninth round Sullivan's telling right-handers on Ryan's jaw and temple, knocked him down all in a heap, and his seconds threw up the sponge.

On January 19, 1885, Ryan again faced Sullivan in a glove contest of four rounds, in New York City. At the end of thirty seconds the police interfered. The two men did not again meet until November 13, 1886, when they were pitted against each other in a glove contest, for the gate receipts, at San Francisco, California. Ryan was knocked out in the third round.

Patrick Ryan was born in the town of Thurles, County Tipperary, Ireland, March 15, 1853. He is six feet one-half inch in height, and his ordinary weight is 221 pounds.

His only battle in the prize-ring, outside of his fight with John L. Sullivan, was with Joe Goss. They fought for $2,000 and the championship of America, at Collier's Station, West Virginia, June 21, 1880. Ryan won in eighty-seven rounds, fought in one hour and twenty-four minutes.

Since his defeat at Mississippi City, Miss., by Sullivan, Ryan has met Joe McAuliffe, in New York City, in a glove contest, and was easily bested.

PADDY RYAN,

The Troy Terror.

THE SULLIVAN-WILSON GLOVE CONTEST.

OE COLLINS, better known as "Tug Wilson," who claimed to be champion of England, was brought to this country by Richard K. Fox, in 1882, especially to fight Sullivan. On July 17th of that year the two men faced each other in a contest with gloves, at the Madison Square Garden, New York City. The big building was crowded, and 5,000 persons clamored loudly for admission after the place was packed. The terms of the contest were that Sullivan should best the Englishman in four three-minute rounds, failing in which he forfeited $1,000 and half of the gate money.

By adopting "falling" tactics, to avoid punishment, Wilson managed to stay out the four rounds, but it was generally conceded that had he stood up and taken his punishment he would have gone down before Sullivan's terrible blows in the third round. As it was he fell to avoid punishment, a slight push was sufficient to send him to the floor.

Harry Hill, who refereed the contest, declared Wilson to be the winner, and with his share of the gate money, the Englishman returned to London, where he opened a public house, out of the profits of which he has accumulated a moderate fortune.

TUG WILSON,

(Joe Collins.)

THE SULLIVAN-MITCHELL CONTEST AND FIGHT.

FTER the champion's failure to conquer Tug Wilson, another young English fighter was brought to this country, in the person of Charley Mitchell, and a glove contest between him and Sullivan was arranged. It came off at Madison Square Garden, New York, on May 4, 1883. Al. Smith was selected as referee, and William J. Mahoney, of Boston, Mass., was elected master of ceremonies.

Although Mitchell displayed unexceptional science, and adopted ring tactics that were altogether new, it is probable that he would have fallen before Sullivan's superior avoirdupois, had not the police interfered in the third round, which saved the plucky young Englishman a knock-out.

The great prize-ring encounter between Sullivan and Mitchell, for £500 a side, London prize ring rules, was fought on Baron Rothschild's training grounds, Apremont, near Chantilly, France, March 10, 1888.

Thirty-nine hard fought rounds, lasting three hours and eleven minutes, found both men exhausted and showing the effects of punishment, and the referee decided that it was a draw. Sullivan stepped into the ring at twenty-five minutes past twelve. In five minutes Mitchell followed. Sullivan wore his Stars and Stripes silk handkerchief, on the left hand corner of which was an Irish harp. The rest of his costume was the same as he always wore at exhibition fights. Mitchell also wore his ordinary exhibition dress. He won the toss for corners and put Sullivan face to the sun and wind, and later to the rain.

The seconds for Mitchell were Jack Baldock, of London, and Jake Kilrain. Sullivan was groomed by George McDonald and Jack Ashton. Jack Barnett was Sullivan's umpire, while Charley Rowell officiated in a similar position for Mitchell. George B. Angle, the stock broker, of London, was referee.

Charley Mitchell was born of Irish parents, in Birmingham, England, November 24, 1861. His first fight was with Bat Cunningham, at Selby Oak, Birmingham, on January 11, 1878, for $25 a side. In fifty minutes he defeated his opponent.

From this time until December, 1882, he met and defeated several good men. On that date in Billy Madden's London Championship Competition, he won all the bouts, and was awarded the champion belt, of massive silver. In the Spring of 1883 he came to this country, and on April 9, 1883, met Mike Cleary in a four-round glove contest, at the American Institute, New York City. He had the best of the contest in the third round when the police interfered.

He fought a draw with Herbert A. Slade, with gloves, at Harry Hill's, Flushing, L. I., October 2, 1883, and on March 26, 1884, bested Joe Denning in a four-round go at Town Hall, New York City. He boxed a draw with Jake Kilrain, at Boston, the following April, and in May met Billy Edwards in a three-round contest, at the Madison Square Garden, New York, which was stopped by the police in the last round.

At Madison Square Garden, New York, October 13, 1884, he was bested by Dominick F. McCaffrey in a four-round glove contest, and on May 16, 1886, he defeated Jack Burke, at Chicago, in a ten-round contest. His next go was with Patsy Cardiff, at Minneapolis, Minn. The men fought with soft gloves and the contest was declared a draw. After this fight he returned to England, and gave boxing exhibitions until the Spring of 1887, when he came back to the United States, and in August of that year met and defeated Steve, or "Reddy" Gallagher, at Cleveland, Ohio.

CHARLIE MITCHELL,
Ex-Champion of England.

THE SULLIVAN-KILRAIN FIGHT.

O N the 7th day of May, 1887, Jake Kilrain, of Baltimore, challenged Sullivan to fight for from $5,000 a side up, and the championship of America, $1,000 forfeit being posted at the office of the New York *Clipper*. This challenge was not accepted, and Sullivan forfeited the title. Later, in 1889, a match was arranged between the two men for $10,000 a side and the championship of the world.

On July 8, 1889, they faced each other in the ring at Richburg, Mississippi, and after fighting seventy-five rounds, occupying two hours, sixteen minutes and twenty-three seconds, Sullivan was declared the winner.

An effort was made by the authorities to stop the fight, and several days thereafter, Sullivan was arrested in New York, on a requisition from Governor Lowry, of Mississippi, and taken to Purvis, that State, for trial. On August 17th following, he was convicted of prize-fighting, and sentenced to one year's imprisonment in the county jail. He appealed the case to the Supreme Court, and was released on $1,500 bail. Kilrain was also arrested in Baltimore and taken to Purvis, but was released on bail to appear for trial.

Jake Kilrain was born in Greenport, Columbia County, N. Y., February 9, 1859. He stands five feet, ten and one-half inches in height, and weighs 230 pounds. He worked in a rolling-mill at Somerville, Mass., and early developed a taste for the manly art, meeting and defeating in turn such men as Jack Daley, Jem Driscoll and Dennis Roach.

In 1883 he became a professional pugilist, and during the next two years met and defeated Harry Allen, Jem McGlynn, William Sheriff, the Prussian, George Godfrey and Jerry Murphy, and fought draws with Jim Goode, George Fryer, Jack Burke and Charley Mitchell. In 1886 he had many adversaries, besting Frank Herald, George Godfrey, Tom Kelly, Denny Killen, Jack Ashton and Joe Lannon.

In June, 1887, Kilrain issued a challenge to fight John L. Sullivan, for $5,000, the *Police Gazette* diamond belt, and the championship of America. Sullivan refused to accept the challenge, and forfeited the title of champion. On December 19, 1887, Kilrain defended the title against Jem Smith, of England, on Isle St. Pierre, France. One hundred and six rounds, lasting two hours and thirty-one minutes, were fought, when darkness intervened. The next day the men met and the fight was declared a draw.

After his defeat by John L. Sullivan, at Richburg, Mississippi, Kilrain, on February 2, 1890, met and defeated Felix Vaquelin for a purse of $3,000. On February 14th he was bested by James J Corbett, in a six-round contest, and on March 13, 1871, at the California Club, San Francisco, he bested George Godfrey in forty-three rounds, for a purse of $5,000. His last battle was with Frank P. Slavin, at the Granite Club, Hoboken, N. J., June 16, 1891. Nine rounds, lasting thirty-three minutes, were fought, when Kilrain was knocked out.

JAKE KILRAIN,

Ex-Champion of the World.

THE SULLIVAN-GREENFIELD GLOVE CONTESTS.

N the night of November 18, 1884, Sullivan met Alfred Greenfield, who claimed to be champion of England, and who had been brought to this country by Richard K. Fox, in a four-round contest with gloves, at Madison Square Garden, New York. It was an international contest, and over $8,000 were taken in at the gate. Charley Johnson, of Brooklyn, N. Y., was selected as referee. Sullivan's timekeeper was Edward Plummer, of *Truth*. The Englishman's interests were looked after by William E. Harding, the sporting editor of the *Police Gazette*.

Greenfield, who was thirty-one years old, measured five feet, ten and one-half inches in height, and weighed one hundred and sixty pounds. Sullivan at the time was twenty-six years old, five feet, ten and one-half inches in height, and weighed one hundred and ninety-eight and one-half pounds. The contest lasted only two rounds, being stopped by the police. Had it been allowed to continue, Sullivan would probably have bested his man. Both men were arrested and tried, but the jury brought in a verdict of not guilty, and they were discharged. Subsequently, on January 12, 1885, the two men met again at Boston, and boxed four rounds, but neither gained the supremacy.

ALF GREENFIELD,
of England.

THE SULLIVAN-SLADE GLOVE CONTEST.

FTER Mitchell had failed to conquer Sullivan, and the latter had refused to meet Mitchell in the twenty-four foot ring for $5,000 a side, Richard K. Fox communicated with Jem Mace, and the latter brought to this country from Australia, a "Maori," named Herbert A. Slade. On August 6, 1883, the Antipodean met Sullivan in a four-round glove contest at Madison Square Garden, New York. Over $8,000 were taken in at the door. Barney Aaron, ex-champion light-weight, was referee. The Maori was over six feet in height and weighed two hundred and one pounds. Sullivan tipped the beam at two hundred and five pounds.

Although so nearly the champion's equal in weight, and with the advantage of greater height, Slade proved an easy "mark" for Sullivan, and demonstrated to everybody's satisfaction that he would never make even a second-class pugilist. At the end of the second round he was knocked to the floor, bleeding from the ears, mouth and nose, and he had to be dragged to his chair. The referee declared Sullivan the winner.

Previous to the contest Richard K. Fox organized a combination of athletes and vaudeville people, styled the "Richard K. Fox, Mace and Slade Combination," and a tour of the country was made. There had been a great deal of newspaper talk about the Maori, and he was thoroughly "boomed" as the coming champion. Promptly upon his arrival in this country Fox agreed to match him against Sullivan for $5,000 a side and the championship of America, but, as had been his previous custom with ambitious pugilists who wished to build up a reputation at the expense of his, the "big fellow" refused to enter the ring of ropes, but agreed to meet Slade in a contest with gloves. Even this recognition of the Maori served to be of great financial benefit to the latter. He is now a policeman at one of the Western summer resorts.

HERBERT A. SLADE,

"The Maori."

THE SULLIVAN-FLOOD FIGHT.

JOHN L. SULLIVAN'S first fight of importance was with John Flood, a heavy weight local boxer of New York. In April, 1881, they agreed to fight according to the rules of the London prize ring, at catch weights, for a purse. The affair was managed by William H. Borst, and took place on the deck of a barge which had been towed up the Hudson river, nearly opposite Yonkers, N. Y., May 16, 1881.

Flood was trained by Bob Smith, and entered the ring weighing 180 pounds. He was twenty-six years of age, and was seconded by Barney Aaron and Dooney Harris. Sullivan was put in condition by Billy Madden, and was seconded by Joe Goss and Madden. Al. Smith was chosen referee, and he announced that the fight would be a perfectly square one for a purse of $1,000, of which amount $750 was to go to the winner.

At 10.40 P.M., time was called and the men faced each other. Both seemed determined to bring the fight to a speedy termination, and fought viciously at close quarters, Sullivan forcing matters. When Flood stepped to the scratch at the beginning of the eighth round, his condition was lamentable, while Sullivan was as fresh as when he entered the ring. One of the future champion's terrible right-handers sent the New Yorker under the ropes, all doubled up, and he was so badly punished that for a time it was feared that he would die. He explained his defeat by saying that he had eaten too much supper. The spectators contributed a purse of $98 to the defeated man, Sullivan presenting him with ten dollars. The fight lasted only sixteen minutes, and demonstrated the fact that Sullivan was a hard hitter and a terrible punisher.

JOHN FLOOD,
New York City.

THE SULLIVAN-TAYLOR GLOVE CONTEST.

THE first man to feel the weight of Sullivan's terrible right in New York City was Steve Taylor. After besting Prof. John Donaldson, in Cincinnati, Sullivan returned to Boston, and expressed his determination of flying for higher game. Billy Madden, the noted pugilist who had charge of Jim Keenan's Boston sporting house, resolved to introduce the "Strong Boy" to the New York public, and Keenan furnished the funds to carry out the arrangement.

Being presented to Richard K. Fox, at the office of the *Police Gazette*, some time in January, 1881, Sullivan expressed a willingness to fight any man in the world, and Mr. Fox was so well pleased with him that he said he would back his visitor to fight any man in the world for $1,000, and would have made a $1,000 champion belt, which he would put up with the stakes.

Sullivan agreed to these terms, and the following week was given a benefit at Harry Hill's. He made an offer on his bills to give $50 to any pugilist who would stand before him four rounds, Marquis of Queensbury rules. This novel proposition created quite a sensation in sporting circles, and after the close of the entertainment Sullivan announced that he was ready to box anybody for the $50.

Steve Taylor, the heavy-weight pugilist, who trained Paddy Ryan when he fought Joe Goss, and who had sparred all over the country with Jem Mace, agreed to face the music. He was seconded by Dick Hollywood, the ex-champion light-weight, while Sullivan was esquired by Billy Madden. Taylor did his best to win, but the heavy sledge-hammer blows of the man from Boston, soon told their usual tale, and Taylor's second threw up the sponge. Sullivan was much elated over his success, and presented Taylor with $25.

STEVE TAYLOR,

New York City.

THE SULLIVAN-DONALDSON FIGHT.

N December, 1880, Sullivan met Prof. John Donaldson, of Cleveland, Ohio, at a boxing exhibition at Cincinnati, and sparred with him. The Bostonian had decidedly the best of the bout, which created great excitement. Donaldson was not satisfied, and he chal-lenged Sullivan to fight with hard gloves for a purse of $500. They met on December 28, 1881, in a room at Cincinnati. Dan Crutchley and Abe Smith, of New York, seconded Donaldson, while Jack Moran and Tom Ryan looked after Sullivan. Patrick Murphy was referee.

Donaldson was whipped from the beginning, but he managed to make the battle last by running all over the ring to avoid Sullivan's terrible blows. The fight lasted through ten rounds when Donaldson was knocked out of time. This was Sullivan's first regular battle, and gave him quite a reputation.

The man who he thus easily defeated stands 5 feet, 10½ inches in height, and weighs in condition 160 pounds. He is well-formed and athletic looking, and when he met Sullivan had figured five times in the ring. He is well known throughout the United States and Canada as a teacher of boxing, and is now Champion Corbett's sparring partner. He is considered a very scientific and clever boxer, and has stood up in bouts with the best of the big ones. Corbett's great success as a ring general is no doubt due to the fact that he has wisely availed himself of the tips given him by the Professor, who is a master of boxing tactics, and believes that brains, coupled with activity and muscle, will, at any time, be more than a match for mere brawn, unbacked by intelligence.

PROF. JOHN DONALDSON,
Cleveland, Ohio.

JOE GOSS.

WHO BATTLED FOR THE CHAMPIONSHIP.

JOE GOSS, who came to this country in 1876 to fight with Tom Allen, who laid claim to the title of champion of America, was born at Northampton, England, November 5, 1838, stood 5 feet 8½ inches in height, and in the old country was wont to fight at 150 pounds.

His first fight was with Jack Rooke, of Birmingham, a brother of George Rooke, whom he defeated September 20, 1859. He followed this victory with others, meeting such men as Tom Price, of Bilston, Bodger Crutchley, Bill Ryall, better known as "Brettle's Big 'Un," Posh Price, Jem Mace, Tom Allen, and Joe Wormald.

Shortly after his arrival in this country Goss issued a challenge which was accepted by Allen, and a match between the two was made for the honors of the championship and $2,500 a side. The men met September 7, 1876, on Kentucky soil, the ring being first pitched in Kenton County, and subsequently, owing to magisterial interference, in Boone County. Twenty-one rounds, occupying forty-eight minutes, were fought, when a decision was given in Goss' favor on a foul.

Goss' last battle was with Paddy Ryan, of Troy, N. Y., for $2,000 and the championship of America. The meet was at Collier Station, West Virginia, June 1, 1880. Owing to the great number of postponements which preceded the fight, Goss trained off, and entered the ring against the Troy giant in an unfit physical condition. After a desperate battle, which lasted one hour and twenty-four minutes, eighty-seven rounds being fought, Ryan was declared the winner.

Goss' defeat created quite a sensation in sporting circles, for no one believed that Ryan, who had never fought in the ring, could whip him. Goss died at Boston, Mass., March 24, 1885, aged forty-six years.

JOE GOSS,
Ex-Champion of America.

THE SULLIVAN-CARDIFF GLOVE CONTEST.

PATSY CARDIFF, the "Peoria Giant," was ambitious to meet Sullivan, and on January 18, 1887, the two men faced each other for a glove contest of six rounds, at the Washington Rink, Minneapolis, Minnesota. The price of admission was fixed at two dollars, and there were over ten thousand spectators. Cardiff, who at that time was twenty-four years of age, trained faithfully for the event, and entered the ring in the pink of condition, weighing 185 pounds.

Sullivan was so confident that he could win an easy victory that he paid little attention to training, but he appeared in fine condition when he entered the ring, weighing 229 pounds. He was seconded by George LeBlanche, the "Marine," while Prof. John Donaldson, of Cincinnati, looked after Cardiff. Billy Wharton, of Minneapolis, was the latter's timekeeper, while Jimmy Murphy held the watch for Sullivan.

The man from Peoria showed himself a plucky fighter, but he was out-classed, and had Sullivan not broken the radius of his left arm during the third round, he would have undoubtedly knocked his man out. At the end of the sixth round there was tremendous excitement, and the immense crowd shouted for a decision. Some yelled for the Peoria man, but their cries were drowned in the louder shouts that went up for Sullivan, to whom the fight was awarded.

Cardiff is of Irish parentage, although he was born in Northern Canada. He is six feet in height, and of gentlemanly manner. He has figured in numerous battles, his most important one being a battle with Jem Goode, the English middle-weight, who was knocked out by him at Chicago, May 25, 1884. He knocked out both Billy Bradburn and Billy Wilson, and fought a draw with Charley Mitchell, having the best of the encounter.

PATSY CARDIFF,
Minneapolis, Minn.

THE SULLIVAN-HERALD GLOVE CONTEST.

FTER Sullivan's contest with Dominick F. McCaffrey, at Cincinnati, he returned to New York, and was matched to box Frank Herald, the "Nicetown Slasher." The police stopped the affair, and another meeting was arranged to take place in Queen's county, Long Island. Again the authorities got wind of the affair, and they were prevented from coming together. Finally arrangements were made for the gladiators to meet in Pittsburgh, Pa., and on September 28, 1886, they faced each other.

Herald weighed 185 pounds, while Sullivan, judging by the contrast between them, must have weighed over 225 pounds. Arthur Chambers and Billy Kelly were Sullivan's seconds, while Benny Jones and Ned Mallahan looked after Herald. Donahue and Comiskey were the timekeepers. The gloves weighed four ounces, and were the same that were used when Sullivan fought John Flood.

In the first round Herald fought a very plucky battle, and although the big fellow used him pretty roughly, he did not show the effects. In the second round Sullivan scored a clean knock down, and was following up his advantage when the police rushed in and with difficulty separated the fighters. Johnny Newell, the referee, declared that Sullivan had the best of the encounter, but Herald was not whipped, and would probably have made a good showing had the contest been allowed to go on.

FRANK HERALD,

"The Nicetown Slasher."

THE SULLIVAN-ELLIOTT GLOVE CONTEST.

ARLY in March, 1882, James Elliott, a native of Athlone, Ireland, who stood 6 feet, 1 inch in height, and weighed 185 pounds, and who had won fame in America by many battles—having fought Jimmy Dunn, Bill Davis, Charley Gallagher, and Johnny Dwyer for the championship—returned to New York and startled the sporting world by declaring himself ready to fight John L. Sullivan. He issued a challenge to that effect on March 30, but Sullivan gave him no attention till the following May, when he agreed to meet him at Washington Park, New York City, and forfeit $500 if he failed to stop him in four three-minute rounds.

Elliott accepted this offer, and the two men met in the ring on the evening of July 4. Mike Cleary, of Philadelphia, was chosen referee. Elliott was seconded by Johnny Roche, while Sullivan was taken care of by Billy Madden. From the very beginning the contest was a one-sided affair, altogether in favor of Sullivan. At the beginning of the third round Elliott came to the scratch decidedly groggy. A blow from Sullivan's terrible right sent him flying into his corner, senseless. The fight lasted seven minutes and twenty seconds, the actual fighting time being five minutes and twenty seconds.

Elliott's first fight was with Nobby Clark. It took place at the Palisades, New Jersey, May 25, 1861, Clark winning after an hour's sharp fight, of 34 rounds. January 6, 1862, Elliott fought Hen Winkle for $500 a side at Bull's Ferry, New Jersey. It was a desperate battle, lasting two hours and fifteen minutes, at the end of which time roughs broke into the ring and the referee declared it a draw. Elliott had decidedly the best of it at the finish.

He afterwards met Jim Dunn, of Brooklyn, at the same place, and after fighting twelve rounds, lasting thirty-five minutes, both men being terribly punished, the referee declared Dunn the winner by a foul. This fight cost Elliott two years in the New Jersey States Prison, he being released June 4, 1865.

Shortly thereafter he challenged any man in the world for from $1,000 to $10,000 a side. Bill Davis, of San Francisco, accepted the challenge, and a match was arranged at $2,000 stakes and the championship of America. The battle took place at Point Pedee, Canada, and lasted eleven rounds. Elliott beat his opponent blind and insensible, and was declared the winner, and champion of America.

He afterwards met Charley Gallagher, for $2,000 a side, at Peach Island, near Detroit, and was declared the winner in twenty-three rounds. On May 9, 1879, at Long Point, Canada, Elliott was beaten by John J. Dwyer, in twelve rounds, lasting twelve minutes forty seconds. Elliott did not figure in any more battles except with gloves, and on March 1, 1883, was fatally shot by Jere Dunn, at Chicago. He was buried in Calvary Cemetery, New York.

JAMES ELLIOTT,

Killed by Jere Dunn.

JACK ASHTON

JOHN L. SULLIVAN'S SPARRING PARTNER.

JOHN, or as he was more familiarly called, "Jack" Ashton, was born in Providence, Rhode Island, in 1863. As a boy he was noted as a big, whole-souled, generous fellow, strong of limb and stout of heart, fond of all out-door sports, and always ready to fight the battles of a friend weaker than himself. It was his cleverness as a fighter that determined him to enter the pugilistic arena, and under competent tutelage he soon became a very proficient boxer.

When he was about eighteen years of age he made his debut in the ring, meeting Jim Dolan, of New York, with whom he fought a draw. From that time on he had many fights, and always made a good showing, either with the gloves or with the naked fists.

Early in 1889 he was matched to fight Joe Lannon to a finish with skin gloves for a purse of $1,500. The event came off at Burrillville, Rhode Island, March 30, and after nineteen desperately fought rounds, Ashton knocked his opponent out. His next fight was with George Godfrey, the colored pugilist, who defeated Ashton in fourteen hard-fought rounds, lasting fifty six minutes. The fight took place at Providence, Rhode Island, November 7, 1889. After the last-mentioned battle Ashton joined forces with John L. Sullivan, becoming the champion's sparring partner. He continued on the road with the big fellow until the time of his death.

After Sullivan's defeat by Corbett at New Orleans, Ashton, who took the ex-champion pugilist's downfall very much to heart, began to dissipate, and neglected his health to such an extent that his friends became alarmed. Shortly after the close of the Christmas holidays in 1892, he was taken sick at the Vanderbilt Hotel, New York City, being finally removed to Bellevue Hospital. Here, at fifteen minutes past nine on the night of January 6, 1893, he breathed his last. Kind friends took charge of his body, and the funeral was held on the following Monday.

Sporting men the world over looked upon Ashton as a good fellow. He made plenty of money, and spent it freely with his associates. As a consequence he was universally popular. Sullivan thought a great deal of him, and the friendship that existed between them was of the closest possible description.

JACK ASHTON,

Sullivan's Sparring Partner.

PETER MAHER,

CHAMPION OF IRELAND.

ETER MAHER was born in County Galway, Ireland, twenty-six years ago. He stands 5 feet, 11½ inches in height, and weighs when in the pink of condition 175 pounds. His first battle was with a big burly countryman, while in the employ of Guinness' brewery, in Dublin. Peter defeated him after a battle lasting two hours and forty minutes. Soon after that he met and defeated J. E. Sullivan, in one round, and Martin O'Hara, in one round, in Tony Sage's amateur competition in the Round Room of the Rotunda, Dublin.

His first professional fight was with Jim O'Doherty, at Dublin. The police interfered, however, in the sixth round. He next met and was defeated in the English middle-weight championships by Bob Heir, and later, being pitted against Alf Bowman, before the Pelican Club easily defeated the latter in five rounds. He met and defeated Gus Lambert in the Pelican Club, London, February 7, 1890, in one quick round, and subsequently was matched to fight Joe McAuliffe before the same club. The authorities refused, however, to allow the fight to go on.

In the fall of 1890 he sailed for this country, arriving in New York City on October 7. Billy Madden, who undertook his management, gave him a royal welcome. A tug was chartered to meet the vessel on which he was a passenger, and he was convoyed up the harbor like a visiting prince, a band of music stationed on the tug playing "Hail to the Chief."

He met and defeated the following men: "Bubbles" Davis, in four rounds; Jim Daly, in one round; Jack Fallon, in two rounds; Sailor Brown, in one round; Jack Smith, in one round, and Fred Woods, of Philadelphia, in one round.

On March 2, 1892, he was bested by Bob Fitzsimmons, in a glove contest, for a purse of $12,000 (£2,400), at New Orleans, La. The fight was of twelve rounds' duration, and lasted forty-seven minutes. On the eighth of the following December he was pitted against Joe Goddard, in the arena of the Coney Island Athletic Club, West Brighton, Coney Island. The contest was with gloves for a purse of $7,500 (£1,500), $1,000 (£200) to go to the loser. In three rounds, lasting eight minutes and fifty seconds, Goddard won the decision.

On the night of May 28, 1894, before upwards of 3,000 people, in the Casino, Boston, Mass., Maher met Geo. Godfrey, the colored heavy-weight, in a glove contest, and after six sharply contested rounds, knocked the latter out.

Maher's last fight was with Frank Craig, the "Harlem Coffee Cooler," in the Music Hall, Boston, Mass., July 16, 1894. Although not in the best of condition he easily defeated Craig in two rounds, lasting four minutes and twenty seconds. On the Saturday following the fight he met Joe Butler before the Ariel Athletic Club, in Philadelphia, in a four-round scientific contest with gloves, and easily won the decision. He is now matched to meet Owen H. Ziegler, who fought a draw with Horace Leeds at Atlantic City.

PETER MAHER,

Champion of Ireland.

FRANK S. CRAIG,

"THE HARLEM COFFEE COOLER."

T was at a boxing tournament at Professor John S. Clark's academy, corner of Eighth and Vine Streets, Philadelphia, where Frank Craig received the title that has clung to him ever since. Denny Butler was the master of ceremonies, and he introduced the various contestants in a humorous speech, giving each some ridiculous title suggested by his exuberant fancy. He introduced Craig as the "Harlem Coffee Cooler," and that he has remained to this day.

Craig is about twenty-six years of age, and in his time he has met some of the best among the heavy-weight pugilists. He has fought twice with Joe Butler, and has always made a creditable showing for science and pluck. His principal contest was with Peter Maher, the Irish champion, July 16, 1894, in the Music Hall, Boston, Mass., he being defeated by the latter in two rounds, lasting four minutes and twenty seconds.

On this occasion Craig weighed 170 pounds, Maher tipping the scales at 180 pounds. Craig was seconded by George Godfrey, Kid Bart, Denny Butler and The. Delaney. Maher was looked after by Billy Hennessey, Sam Fitzpatrick and Patsey Kerrigan. The hall was crowded, over three thousand enthusiastic lovers of the manly art being present, and the greatest enthusiasm prevailed.

It is predicted by sporting men who have carefully watched the "Coffee Cooler's" career, that he has a brilliant future before him, and may yet reach a position on the ladder of pugilistic fame very near the top. He is a fine-looking, athletic-built man, straight as an arrow, with long arms and legs, a tapered waist, full chest and broad shoulders. He hits hard, is quick of movement, and displays skilful generalship in avoiding the blows of an antagonist.

Some time after his unsuccessful contest with Maher he sailed for England, being matched to fight O'Brien, the Welsh champion, before the National Sporting Club, of London.

FRANK CRAIG,

"The Harlem Coffee Cooler."

"SPARROW" GOLDEN,

PHILADELPHIA.

AMES, better known in pugilistic circles as "Sparrow" Golden, was born in the old Kensington District, Philadelphia, about thirty-eight years ago. He comes of a fighting family, two of his brothers having won no little distinction as boxers of scientific merit.

Golden's early training for his after contests in the ring was received along the Richmond coal wharves, where every other man is a boxer. He bested the majority of those who pitted themselves against him, and finally entered the field as a full-fledged pugilist. For several years he appeared nightly at the various boxing resorts which then flourished in the Quaker City, and several times was matched for small purses on the outside.

His most notable contest was with Lew Cramer, whom he met with hard gloves, near Germantown, Pa., for a purse of $500 (£100). It was a sharply contested fight, Golden having the best of it from the start. In the ninth round Cramer was knocked out.

After this fight Golden's star rose considerably in the pugilistic firmament. Sporting men thought he had the making of a first-class fighter, and in time might meet the champion. Accordingly, in the winter of 1885, he was matched to meet Dominick F. McCaffrey, who had recently fought six rounds with John L. Sullivan.

The contest was to a finish, and was fought near Fort Hamilton, Long Island. A crowd of Boston, New York, Philadelphia, Baltimore and Pittsburg sporting men were present. Some difficulty was experienced in eluding the authorities, but the ring was finally pitched, and just at day-break the two men faced each other. Both were in the pink of condition, but it was seen from the start that Golden was outclassed. He could not stand against the terrific rushes and vicious blows of the Pittsburger, and went down.

After this fight Golden relinquished boxing as a pursuit, and returned to his old work about the coal wharves. Finally he drifted South and West, and when last heard from was in Minneapolis, Minnesota.

"SPARROW" GOLDEN,

Philadelphia, Pa.

GEORGE GODFREY,

FIRST COLORED HEAVY-WEIGHT CHAMPION OF AMERICA.

THE first colored heavy-weight champion of America, who won his title by skilful generalship, undoubted courage and more than ordinary science, is George Godfrey, of Boston, Mass. He was born on Prince Edward's Island, March 20, 1853. He stands 5 feet 10½ inches in height, and when in condition weighs 170 pounds. He has won many fights, fought several to a draw, and been defeated but rarely.

His first battle was with Ham Williams, in 1882, whom he defeated in seven minutes of hot fighting. He next defeated Professor Hadley in four rounds, for a stake of $100 (£20), following this battle, in 1884, by whipping Jimmy Doherty in one round, lasting one minute and twenty-five seconds, for a purse of $150 (£30).

After defeating Barney Small, in two rounds, for $25 (£5) a side, Godfrey had another meeting with Professor Hadley, which resulted in a draw. On May 10, 1884, he met McHenry Johnson, the "Black Star," at Boston, Mass., but the police interfered and stopped the fight, with Godfrey decidedly in the lead.

In 1887 he fought a six-round draw with Joe Lannon, and on August 24, 1888, at the California Athletic Club, San Francisco, was defeated by Peter Jackson. The fight was for a purse of $2,000 (£400), and was won by Jackson in nineteen rounds, lasting one hour and fifteen minutes. Godfrey then met and defeated Jack Ashton, at Providence, R. I., on November 7, 1889, in fourteen rounds, lasting fifty-six minutes.

His most important battle was with McHenry Johnson, the "Black Star," for a purse of $850 (£170), at Bloomfield, Boulder County, Colorado, January 25, 1888. Godfrey had his man whipped in the third round, but Johnson was allowed to face him again, and was knocked out by a blow that would have felled an ox. It was claimed that this blow was a foul one, and the referee so decided, but the Denver Crib Club, under whose auspices the fight was held, decided that no foul had been committed. Godfrey was given $150 (£30) for expenses and $600 (£120) of the purse, while Johnson received $150 (£30) and $100 (£20) for expenses.

Godfrey's next fight was with "Denver Ed" Smith, the police interfering. On March 13, 1891, Godfrey met Jake Kilrain in a glove contest for a purse of $5,000 (£1,000), at San Francisco, California. After forty-four rounds of good hard fighting Kilrain succeeded in knocking his man out. The battle lasted two hours and fifty-five minutes.

Godfrey defeated Joe Lannon on May 16, 1892, at West Brighton, Coney Island, in four rounds, lasting fifteen minutes, for a purse of $3,000 (£600), and was in turn defeated on October 31, following, by Joe Choynski, at the same place, in fifteen rounds, lasting fifty-nine minutes, for a purse of $5,000 (£1,000).

In a glove contest in the Casino, Boston, Mass., May 28, 1894, Godfrey was knocked out by Peter Maher, in the sixth round, after one of the greatest battles seen in Boston for years.

GEORGE GODFREY,
Colored Champion Heavy Weight.

WILLIAM SHERIFF,

"THE PRUSSIAN."

WILLIAM SHERIFF, better known as "The Prussian," was born in Leicestershire, England, about forty-seven years ago. He early developed a taste for boxing, and by the time he was thirty years of age had met several good men, and established for himself a splendid record for courage and ability to stand and give punishment.

In the early 80's his reputation had extended even to this country, and Arthur Chambers, the ex-light-weight champion, of Philadelphia, thought that he might be a worthy foe to pit against the then champion, John Lawrence Sullivan. Accordingly he entered into negotiations with Sheriff, and an agreement was made between the two men, whereby the Prussian visited this country and placed himself under Chambers' management.

It was thought expedient to test Sheriff's ability in a contest with some of the minor lights of the prize ring, and several contests were arranged. In all of these "The Prussian" made a very creditable showing, but it was discovered that he lacked the science and other fighting qualities necessary to make him a champion, and in the latter part of 1892 he returned to England again.

He had been suffering for some time with a disabled leg, and this rapidly grew worse after his arrival in London. His old ring friends rallied to his support, seeing to it that he wanted for none of the comforts of life and the best surgical attendance. He failed rapidly, however, despite these attentions, dying finally at the house of a friend in London, England, June 4, 1893.

His most notable contests in this country were with Mike Cleary, who knocked him out twice in Philadelphia, and Jake Kilrain, who did the same service for him in Boston. On April 10, 1884, at Philadelphia, Pa., he met John Welch, in a finish fight with hard gloves, Marquis of Queensbury rules, for a purse of $500 (£100). In this contest Sheriff made his best showing. Seventy-six rounds, lasting over five hours, were fought, at the end of which time the referee declared the contest a draw.

Sheriff's fighting weight was a trifle beyond the middle-weight limit. When he met Welch he weighed 158 pounds, and was in the pink of condition. This contest was one of the longest on record, and showed conclusively that while lacking in many other essential qualifications of a pugilist, "The Prussian" had an abundant supply of grit and bull-dog tenacity of purpose.

WILLIAM SHERIFF,
"The Prussian."

FRANCIS PATRICK SLAVIN,

OF AUSTRALIA.

RANCIS PATRICK SLAVIN was born of Irish parents at Maitland, New South Wales, Australia, in 1862. He stands 5 feet, 10½ inches in height, measures 43½ inches around the chest, and in condition weighs about 190 pounds. He was apprenticed when a lad to the trade of blacksmithing, but soon forsook the anvil for the more adventurous life of a gold digger. He soon figured in athletic sports and acquired a good reputation as a runner and walker.

In 1885 he left New South Wales and went to Queensland, where he first appeared as a boxer, making his debut in the ring by beating Martin Powers in thirteen minutes in a match for $250 (£50) a side. He afterwards met and defeated Tom Burke, in four rounds; Shannon, of Gympia, in two rounds; Sam Burke, of Rockhampton, in ten rounds; Prof. Bables, in a round and a half; Tom Taylor, in a round and a half; and Jem Fogarty, "The Jaw Breaker," in three rounds. He also fought a draw with Martin Costello.

Upon the arrival of Jack Burke, the "Irish Lad," in Australia, in 1889, he and Slavin were matched for a finish fight, which came off February 4, 1889. Burke was outclassed, and was easily defeated in eight rounds. After this battle Slavin sailed for England, where he was immediately matched with Bill (Chesterfield) Goode. This fight came off October 17, 1889, at Westminster Bridge Road, London, and was for $2,000 (£400) a side. Goode was knocked out in the third round.

He was immediately matched with Jem Smith, champion of England, the contest ending in a wrangled draw at Bruges, Belgium, December 23, 1889. It was for $1,000 (£200) a side. Joe McAuliffe was his next opponent. They met before the Ormonde Club, London, England, September 27, 1890, for a purse of $5,000 (£1,000) and the International Championship Belt. McAuliffe lasted one and a half rounds, occupying six minutes.

In the spring of 1891 Slavin came to this country, and was immediately matched to meet Jake Kilrain. The fight was with gloves for a purse of $10,000 (£2,000), to be equally divided. It came off June 27, 1891, at Hoboken, New Jersey, Slavin winning in nine rounds, lasting thirty-five minutes. Returning to England he was matched in a glove contest with Peter Jackson, for a purse of $12,500 (£2,500). The contest came off May 30, 1892, at London, England, Jackson winning in ten rounds, lasting thirty-nine minutes. On May 29, 1893, he met Jim Hall, in a glove contest for $13,500 (£2,700), at London, England, being defeated by the latter in seven rounds, lasting twenty-seven minutes.

Slavin has expressed his determination of challenging the winner in the Corbett-Jackson fight, if the two men ever meet, but on September 8, 1894, he refused to meet "Pony" Moore's Unknown, supposed to be Charley Mitchell, and his backer withdrew the forfeit of $5,000 (£1,000).

FRANK (PADDY) SLAVIN,
Australia.

JAMES DALY,

CHAMPION HEAVY-WEIGHT OF PENNSYLVANIA.

JAMES DALY, at one time champion heavy-weight of Pennsylvania, and a fighter of no mean importance, is well known as the sparring partner of Champion James J. Corbett, during his exhibitions prior to and after his battle for the championship with John L. Sullivan. Daly was one of Corbett's trainers for that celebrated battle, and stood behind the young champion in the ring at New Orleans. He is now athletic instructor of the Buffalo (New York) Athletic Club.

Daly is a Philadelphian by birth, having been born March 25, 1867, at Third and Dauphin Streets, that city. He was always active and fond of athletic sports, and being a good rough and tumble fighter, was the leader among the boys in his neighborhood. When he was yet a lad he learned the contortion business and was one of the three famous Majiltons, who travelled extensively in this country, he taking the part of the girl. He was with them from 1883 to 1885, when he severed his connection and did a contortion act by himself.

In the latter part of 1886 he came back to Philadelphia and gained considerable renown by meeting and defeating all comers at the various boxing halls which at that time flourished in the Quaker City. He is also famous as a wrestler, having met some of the most noted athletes in that branch of the business, including Jack Carkeek, Jack Hart and Jack Murray.

In 1888 Daly travelled with Muldoon, the wrestler, and met all comers, with unvarying success, as "Muldoon's Unknown." In the fall of 1890 Daly became Corbett's sparring partner, continuing with the champion until some time after the fight with Sullivan. His four-round battles have been many, and he has only met with four defeats, once by Denny Kelliher, after he (Daly) had fought thirteen of the fifteen rounds contested with a broken hand, once after his fight with Ed Smith had been stopped in the seventh round by the police, and after palpable fouling by Smith, when the referee decided that Smith was the winner, again in his fight with Peter Maher, before the Ariel Club in Philadelphia, when Maher knocked him through the ropes and the referee counted him out before he could get into the ring again, and the last time in his fight with Joe Butler, at Coney Island.

He has fought draws with John Fallon, the Brooklyn strong boy, and with Denny Kelliher, of Boston, and has met and defeated the following: Ed. Conners, Bill Gabig, Bob Farrel, Tom Green, Tom Kelly, J. Harrington, Pete Riley, Jack Stewart, Jack Ballard, Jack Murray, Jack Tracey, Jack Trainor, Bill Brown, Jack Horace, Mike Cunningham, Jack Brennan, Dick Harrington, Mike Boden, Bob Caffey, Mike Monaghan, Bill Kraemer, and Pat Farrell.

Joe McAuliffe failed to knock him out in six rounds, as he agreed to do, and the only notable defeat that he has met with was when in a glove contest for a purse of $2,500 (£500), at West Brighton, Coney Island, June 22, 1893, he was bested by Joe Butler, the colored pugilist, in six rounds.

JIM DALY,

Philadelphia, Pa.

CAPT. JAMES C. DAILEY,

KNOCKED OUT BY CORBETT IN FOUR ROUNDS.

APT. JAMES C. DAILEY, who is often spoken of as the Apollo of the prize ring, is best known on the Pacific Slope, where he has for years figured as a teacher of scientific boxing. His friends say that he is too pleasant and agreeable a gentleman, and has too much kindness of heart to make a successful fighter, where the ability to deliver and take hard blows is the prime requisite.

He has fought several ring fights, however, and in 1885, when James J. Corbett had just begun to attract attention as a rising young pugilist, he met the coming champion, and managed to stand up against him for four rounds. He has hosts of friends in California, and some of the best fighters that the Pacific Slope has developed, first learned the mysteries of scientific boxing under his tutelage.

Personally, Capt. Dailey is the *beau ideal* of manly beauty. He has a handsome face, clean-cut limbs, a deep chest, and broad shoulders. His manners are polished and agreeable, and he wins friends rapidly. As an exponent of scientific boxing he has few superiors in this country. He was born of Irish parents in San Francisco, about thirty-two years ago, and has made that city his home ever since.

After his contest with Corbett he predicted for the latter a brilliant future, and in an interview on the result of his contest with Gentleman Jim, said: "That man Corbett is a wonder. He is strong, quick and courageous, and these qualities are necessary in a successful ring fighter. His hitting powers are tremendous, and he is scientific enough to avoid the blows of an opponent. He is young, and has not yet attained his full physical development. Seven or eight years hence, if he takes good care of himself, and I think he will, for he appears to have a very level head, he will be in his prime. Then, if he don't knock out every man that faces him, I'm no judge."

This prediction was made in 1885, when Corbett was but nineteen years of age. How truly the genial Captain's words have been verified, the facts of history attest. Corbett has reached his prime, and he has defeated every man that has been pitted against him.

CAPT. J. C. DAILEY,
San Francisco, Cal.

JOE McAULIFFE.

CALIFORNIA.

JOE McAULIFFE, the big-hearted and big-bodied pride of the Pacific Slope, has been phenomenally successful in his battles. His first ring fight was with Martin Costello, the Australian, in San Francisco, which he won in four rounds. He subsequently defeated Jack Brady, heavy-weight champion of California, and Dick Matthews, whom he put to sleep in seven rounds.

This latter battle made him champion of the Pacific Coast. He next met Mike Brennan, the "Port Costa Giant," in a forty-nine round battle before the California Athletic Club, and defeated the latter. The next man to meet McAuliffe was Paddy Ryan, who was whipped in three rounds, McAuliffe not receiving a blow. He then defeated Frank Glover in forty-nine rounds of terrific fighting, during which, in the first round, he broke the small bone of his right hand.

His next battle was with Mike Conley, the "Ithaca Giant," for a $2,000 (£400) purse, October 26, 1888, before the California Athletic Club, which he won in two rounds. December 23, 1888, he met his first defeat at the hands of Peter Jackson, before the California Athletic Club, for a purse of $3,500 (£700), Jackson winning in twenty-four rounds. After this McAuliffe beat Tom Lees, for a purse of $2,000 (£400), before the Golden Gate Athletic Club, San Francisco, knocking his opponent out in eight rounds.

On September 11, 1889, he met and defeated Pat Killen, the champion of the northwest, at San Francisco, California, for a purse of $2,500 (£500), in seven rounds, lasting twenty-seven minutes. On September 27, 1890, before the Ormonde Club, London, England, he had an international glove contest for a purse of $5,000 (£1,000), and a belt, with F. P. Slavin, and was defeated by the latter in two rounds, lasting six minutes. He was also defeated by Joe Goddard on June 30, 1892, at San Francisco, California, for a purse of $5,000 (£1,000), Goddard winning after fifteen rounds, lasting fifty-nine minutes.

JOE McAULIFFE,

California.

JIM FELL.

ENGLAND.

IM FELL was born in England about 1856, and made his first appearance in the fistic arena there, where he won some fame and money as a gamey and scientific fighter. Coming to this country, he selected Saginaw, Michigan, as his base of operations, and has met some of the most noted pugilists in the country. He weighs 190 pounds, and measures five feet, ten and one-half inches in height.

He has traveled extensively over the country, and has made a good record as a plucky and skilful boxer. He fought twice with John P. Clow, the middle-weight pugilist, who was shot dead by F. C. Marshall, in Denver, Colorado, December 9, 1890, scoring a victory on both occasions.

He has also met Patsey Cardiff, "Denver" Ed. Smith, Frank Glover, Mike Conley, "The Ithaca Giant," C. C. Smith, of Saginaw, and others, and in every battle, whether a victor or defeated, has acquitted himself with credit.

JIM FELL,

England.

JEM SMITH,

EX-CHAMPION OF ENGLAND.

JEM SMITH, ex-champion of England, was born January 21, 1853, in Red Lion Market, White Cross Street, St. Luke's, London. He is five feet, eight and one-half inches in height. For some years he was employed in one of the London timber yards, but developing a taste for boxing, he was taken in hand by Jack Knifton and the veteran Goode, and later by F. Grim, of the Central Club. His first success was in a competition at the Griffin, Shoreditch. Later he beat Snowey, of Holloway, and then for a purse of $50 (£10), Harry Arnold.

He forfeited $5 (£1) for a match with Jack Massey, and then met Woolf Bendoff, with gloves, for $100 (£20) a side, at an East End Club. Smith injured his arm in this contest, but was declared the winner. He next defeated Jack Wannop and Tom Longer. Smith's battle with Jack Davis, for $500 (£100) a side, was with bare knuckles, and came off on the borders of Surrey and Sussex, December 17, 1885. Six rounds, occupying seven minutes and fifty-six seconds, were fought, when Davis was knocked out.

Smith's next battle was with Alf Greenfield, for $1,500 (£300) a side and the championship. The fight took place at Maisons Lafitte, near Paris, February 17, 1886. In the thirteenth round the ropes were cut and the ring broken into, Smith having the best of the contest. On December 1, 1886, he was matched with Jack Knifton, but the fight never came off.

On December 19, 1887, Smith fought with Jake Kilrain, on the Island of St. Pierre, France, for the championship of the world and $5,000 (£1,000) a side. For two hours and a half the two men battled, 106 rounds being fought. The fight was finally stopped by darkness, and a draw was agreed upon. Subsequently, November 11, 1889, before the Pelican Club, London, he faced Peter Jackson in a glove contest, for a purse of $5,000 (£1,000), Jackson winning the decision in two rounds, on a claim of foul.

Smith's last contest was with Frank P. Slavin, at Bruges, Belgium, in December, 1889. Fourteen rounds were fought, and the friends of Slavin declared that he did not receive fair play, and had decidedly the best of the contest. The referee, through fear, declared the fight a draw, but public opinion awarded the battle to Slavin, and Smith thought it best to permanently retire from the ring.

JEM SMITH,

England.

MIKE CLEARY.

PHILADELPHIA.

IKE CLEARY was born in the County Queens, Ireland, in the year 1858. While quite a lad he emigrated to this country and settled in Philadelphia, where he learned the trade of horse-shoeing. Being possessed of an inherent love of athletic sports, he indulged his disposition in this regard by taking part in the various boxing exhibitions which took place in his adopted city, where for several years he kept a saloon on Vine Street, between Eighth and Ninth, and afterwards on Walnut Street above Eighth.

His first essay in the ring was with Weeden, the English pugilist, whom he defeated after a plucky engagement of thirty-eight rounds, lasting one hour and thirty-eight minutes. His most notable essay with the gloves was at the Alhambra Theatre, New York, October 18, 1882, the occasion being a benefit to George Rooke, the middle-weight champion. Rooke had announced that he would give any pugilist, barring Sullivan, $50 (£10), who would stop him in four rounds. Cleary took up the offer and so completely worsted Rooke, knocking him out three times, that in the third round, after one or two terrific right-handers, the middle-weight was floored, and lay insensible for fifteen minutes.

After this showing Cleary was hailed as a very clever boxer, and he adopted pugilism as a profession. On May 22, 1885, he fought a draw with Charley Mitchell, at San Francisco, California, the police interfering in the fourth round. On November 23, the same year, he faced Jack Burke, the "Irish Lad," in San Francisco, California. The men fought nine rounds when the police interfered, and the contest was declared a draw. On the twenty-eighth of the following month, Cleary and Burke again came together in Chicago, Illinois, Cleary being defeated in three rounds.

In the fall of 1892, in New York City, while attempting to board a horse car while in motion, Cleary met with an accident which resulted in the amputation of his right foot. On November 27, following, he was tendered a monster benefit at the Lenox Opera House, Thirty-Fourth Street near Fourth Avenue, on which occasion the leading pugilistic lights of the country appeared. A handsome sum was realized for th relief of the maimed pugilist, and he retired to Belfast, New York, where he died, September 5, 1893.

MIKE CLEARY,

Philadelphia.

MIKE CONLEY,

"THE ITHACA GIANT."

IKE CONLEY, better known under the sobriquet of "The Ithaca Giant," was born in the upper part of Pennsylvania, near the line of New York State, about 1859. When quite a lad his parents moved to Ithaca, New York, and it was here that Mike learned sparring and developed into a hard hitter and a very clever pugilistic general.

When pugilism had its home in Philadelphia, in 1883–4, Conley journeyed to the Quaker City, and selected Prof. John S. Clark as his patron and pugilistic manager. At Clark's Academy he proved a great attraction, and during one season met and stopped no less than twenty-one men in four-round bouts. Only two of the fighters that were pitted against him managed to last out the four rounds, Mike Boden, "The Canuck," and Billy Gabig, "The Mysterious Boxer."

Emboldened by his success among the Quaker City boxers, Conley started out for new worlds to conquer. His first match was with Frank Herald, "The Nicetown Slasher," in New York City, Herald knocking him out in one round. He afterwards met Joe McAuliffe, in San Francisco, and was defeated in two rounds. Undismayed by his bad luck, he made a match with Billy Woods, in New Orleans, and for the third time was beaten, Woods knocking him out in the second round.

This latter battle was his last. He settled down in Memphis, Tennessee, and with the money he had saved from his sparring contests, opened a hotel, which he still conducts. Conley measures six feet in height, and fights at 180 pounds.

MIKE CONLEY,

"The Ithaca Giant."

TOM ALLEN.

ENGLAND.

TOM ALLEN was born in Birmingham, England, in April, 1840. He stands five feet, nine and one-half inches in height, and weighs at the present time in the neighborhood of 200 pounds. In fighting condition he tipped the beam at 175 pounds. His first battle was with Waggoner, of Birmingham, $25 (£5) a side, in the autumn of 1861, which Waggoner won. Six months later he met Young Gould for $100 (£20) a side, and the latter won. Posh Price whipped Allen in fifty-five minutes in July, 1862. Allen's next engagement was with Bingley Rose, of Nottingham, England, for $125 (£25) a side, whom he conquered in ten rounds, lasting twenty-nine minutes, January, 1864.

Some six months later, Bob Smith, the "Liverpool Black," whipped Allen in two hours and fifteen minutes. He then fought Jack Parkinson, whom he "cut into ribbons" in twenty minutes, for $125 (£25) a side. Meeting Posh Price a second time, for $125 (£25) a side, the two men fought forty-one rounds, lasting two hours and five minutes, in November, 1865. Allen had decidedly the best of the fight, and as Price gave a tip to the police and had himself arrested, the stakes were given to Allen.

On June 12, 1866, Allen defeated George Iles, and on March 5, 1867, fought a draw with Joe Goss for $500 (£100) a side. The fight took place in Monmouthshire, and lasted one hour and fifty-two minutes, in which time thirty-five rounds were fought. Allen afterwards received two forfeits of $250 (£50) each from Bill Thorpe, Peter Millard and Mike Cocklin.

Allen came to this country in July, 1867, and his first fight was with Bill Davis, at Chateau Island, St. Louis, January 12, 1869, when he won in forty-three rounds. On February 23, 1869, he fought Charley Gallagher at Carroll Island, near St. Louis, and was knocked out by the latter in the second round, after fighting but three minutes. On July 15, 1869, he fought Mike McCoole on Foster's Island, in the Mississippi river, for $1,000 (£200) a side, and the excursion money. Nine rounds were fought, and Allen made a chopping-block of his opponent. A crowd broke into the ring, and the referee gave the decision to McCoole. He again met Charley Gallagher, at Foster's Island, near St. Louis, August 17, 1869, and although he had Gallagher whipped in the eleventh round, after twenty-five minutes of sharp fighting, the referee decided in favor of the latter. On May 10, 1870, he fought Jem Mace at Kennerville, near New Orleans, for $5,000 (£1,000) and the championship of the world. Mace won in ten rounds, lasting forty minutes.

On September 23, 1873, he fought Mike McCoole again, for $2.000 (£400) at Chateau Island, St. Louis, Allen being declared the winner after twenty-nine rounds, lasting twenty minutes, had been fought. He afterwards fought a draw with Ben Hogan, the reformed preacher-pugilist, near Council Bluffs. His last fight was with Joe Goss for the championship of America and $5,000 (£1,000), in Kentucky, in 1876. The men fought in two rings, the first being erected in Kent, and the second in Boone county. Twenty-one rounds were fought in fifty-three minutes, when Goss was declared the winner by a foul. Allen was arrested and put under bonds. He afterwards settled down in St. Louis, where he still lives.

TOM ALLEN,

England.

"DENVER" ED. SMITH.

ENGLAND.

EDWARD, better known as "Denver" Smith, was born in Birmingham, England, March 17, 1865. He stands five feet, ten and one-half inches, and fights at 175 pounds. He is a brother of Paddy Smith, who trained Jimmy Carroll to fight Jack McAuliffe in San Francisco. Smith first entered the fistic arena under the tutelage of Jem Mace, with whom he toured for three years. During this time he had thirty-six battles, in all of which he was declared the victor.

His most important fight in England was with Charley Mitchell, with whom he battled for one hour and forty minutes, when the police interfered and the contest was declared a draw. Smith came to America in 1884, in company with George Fryer and Alf Greenfield. He had an engagement of six weeks at Prof. John S. Clark's Club Theatre, in Philadelphia, during which time he met and knocked out all comers. Going to Baltimore he defeated Jim O'Day, Denny Shay and Dick Roberts. In New York he defeated Tommy Chandler, of Boston, Dooney Harris, Tom Henry, of Manchester, England, and Jimmie Murphy. He next went to Chicago and defeated Jimmie Conley, of Boston, in five rounds.

Smith then joined the "Jack Burke Combination," which was touring the country, as "The Irish Lad's" sparring partner. His first battle in this country was with John P. Clow, the champion of the northwest. The two men fought ten desperate rounds, when the contest was declared a draw. Smith's next fight was with Sam Matthews, the heavy-weight champion of the Pacific Coast, whom he defeated in six rounds. He then defeated Jack Ingle, the "Butcher Boy," of Minneapolis, Minn., in three rounds, at Italy, Montana, and Dan Gallagher, in three rounds, at Butte, Montana.

Smith went to Denver, Colorado, on October 13, 1888, where he knocked out Lawrence Farrell, (William Keough) in two rounds. On February 22, 1889, at Denver, Colorado, he met George LeBlanche, "The Marine," for a purse of $2,500 (£500). In the second round the police interfered, Smith having the best of the contest. A few months later Smith went to Hot Springs, Arkansas, and fought Mike Cleary, knocking him out in one round. Afterwards he defeated Peter Dailey, of Philadelphia, and was bested by Peter Jackson and George Godfrey.

His most important fight was with Joe Goddard, at New Orleans, La., March 3, 1893, for a purse of $10,000 (£2,000). The battle was with gloves, eighteen rounds, lasting one hour and ten minutes, at the end of which time Smith was declared the winner.

October 3, 1894, Smith fought six rounds with Lawrence Farrell (William Keough), about twenty miles from Denver, on the Gulf road. After repeated fouling on the part of Farrell, and several warnings from the referee, in the sixth round Farrell again fouled Smith and threw him over the ropes, when the referee gave Smith the fight. Smith wanted to fight it out, but his friends would not let him. Omar Anderson, Paddy Smith and Joe Mulvihill were Smith's seconds, and Tom West, Billy Thomas and Bat Masterson seconded Farrell; Harry Stewart and "Soapy" Smith were time-keepers, and Reddy Gallagher was referee.

"DENVER" ED SMITH,

England.

JACK WELCH.

PHILADELPHIA.

JACK WELCH was born in that home of pugilists, Birmingham, England, about 1854. Being of athletic build, and with a natural bent for sport of a physical nature, he early developed into a boxer, and by the time he had reached his prime had met some of the best of British fighters. He came to this country in 1884, and was one of the star attractions at Prof. John S. Clark's Academy, Eighth and Vine Streets, Philadelphia.

While here he stopped Jack Keefe twice in four-round glove contests, and being pitted against Dominick F. McCaffrey, the latter agreed to forfeit $250 if he did not stop the Birmingham man in four rounds. He failed to do this, and the showing then made by Welch brought about his meeting with William Sheriff, "The Prussian," who had been brought to this country as a possible champion by Arthur Chambers.

A purse of $500 (£100) was raised, and the battle came off at Germantown, Philadelphia, April 10, 1884. The contest was with hard gloves, Marquis of Queensbury rules, and was one of the longest fought and most stubbornly contested battles in the history of the prize ring. Seventy-six rounds, lasting over five hours, were fought, at the end of which time the referee declared a draw.

After this contest Welch virtually retired from pugilism, except to indulge in an occasional friendly go, and several years ago he settled down at Newark, New Jersey, where he conducts a very profitable and popular saloon. Welch measures five feet, 11 inches in height, and in fighting condition weighs 160 pounds.

JACK WELCH,

Philadelphia.

BOB FITZSIMMONS,

CHAMPION MIDDLE WEIGHT OF THE WORLD.

FITZSIMMONS was born in Cornwall, England, June 14, 1862. He stands five feet, eleven and three-quarter inches in his stocking feet, and weighs 165 to 168 pounds, out of condition. He made his first reputation by knocking out Herbert A. Slade, "The Maori." He made quite a record by knocking out many clever fighters in Australia, and then went to America.

Ever since Fitzsimmons has held the interest of the American sporting world, and at no time has he stood so high as now, that he is matched to fight the heavy weight champion of the world, James J. Corbett.

His first appearance in the ring was at Jem Mace's amateur boxing tournament, at Timaru, New Zealand, eleven years ago (1883). He succeeded in knocking out four men that night, winning the amateur championship of New Zealand, and a gold watch.

The next year Mace visited New Zealand, and gave another tournament. Fitzsimmons knocked out five men that night, after which he put on the gloves with Herbert Slade, and to every one's surprise, "bested him."

His next fight was with Arthur Cooper, under London Prize Ring rules, at Timaru, defeating him in three rounds. Then he fought Jack Murphy, and defeated him in four rounds. Then Jim Crawford, who was defeated in three rounds. Both fights were under London Prize Ring rules, and both men were "knocked out."

After this he left New Zealand and went to Sydney, sparring for the first time there, at Larry Foley's Athletic Hall, where he defeated Bramsmead, a heavy weight, in two rounds; he weighed 170 pounds. Fitzsimmons at this time weighed 148 pounds. He next defeated Jack Greentree, a middle weight, at Foley's, in three rounds. Dick Sandal, who became amateur champion after Fitzsimmons left New Zealand, was defeated by him in four rounds. Bill Slavin was the next to succumb; then Enger, who had fought a draw with "Starlight," the colored middle weight champion of Australia, was defeated. Then Conway, the champion of Ballarat, in three rounds.

Dick Ellis was beaten in three rounds. Jim Hall, middle weight champion of Australia and Queensland, was beaten in five rounds. "Starlight" was knocked out in nine rounds. His last fight in Australia was with Prof. West, a heavy weight; he was knocked out in two minutes.

His first fight in America was in San Francisco, with Billy McCarthy. Fitzsimmons knocked him out in nine rounds. He then met Arthur O. Upham, before the Audubon Club, New Orleans, and defeated him in five rounds.

Fitzsimmons was then matched to fight Jack Dempsey, for the middle weight championship of the world. The fight took place before the Olympic Club, of New Orleans, January 14, 1891. Fitzsimmons "knocked out" Dempsey in thirteen rounds. On March 2, 1892, "Fitz" defeated Peter Maher, in twelve rounds, before the Olympic Club, New Orleans. A year later, 1893, Jim Hall was "knocked out," in four rounds. His fight with Joe Choynski was declared a draw. "Fitz" defeated Dan Creedon, of Australia, in two rounds, at the Olympic Club, New Orleans, September 26, 1894. Time, four minutes.

BOB FITZSIMMONS,

Champion Middle Weight of the World.

DAN CREEDON.

AUSTRALIA.

DAN CREEDON, who won the middle weight championship of Australia, in a series of hard-fought battles, was born in New Zealand, in June, 1868. He weighs from 158 to 160 pounds, and stands five feet, nine and one-half inches in height. He is clever, a terrific hitter, can take a great deal of punishment, and his fighting is of the rushing, aggressive style. In manner he is quiet and unassuming, and he is jolly and good-natured in private, although possessed of a bull-dog like ferocity in the ring.

His Australian record is an undefeated one, and is as follows: Beat Owen Daley in eight rounds; fought thirty-three rounds with Pat Ryan; had an eight-round draw with Jim Hall; defeated Jim Watts, in five rounds; won the middle weight belt, offered by the Melbourne Club, October 16, 1891; fought Martin Costello twice, defeating him once and making a twenty-three-round draw with him the next time; defeated Jim Ryan, the Sydney heavy weight, in seven rounds; defeated Mike Dunn, the Sydney middle weight, in two rounds.

In 1893 Creedon went to America, and on August 14th, of that year, for a purse of $9,000 (£1,800), fought and defeated Alec. Greggains, of San Francisco, at Roby, Indiana, in fifteen rounds, lasting fifty-five minutes. His display of generalship and tremendous hitting-powers on that occasion, brought about a match with Bob Fitzsimmons, at 154 pounds, for $5,000 (£1,000) and the middle weight championship of the world.

The great battle was fought in the Olympic Club, New Orleans, September 26, 1894, for a purse of $5,000 (£1,000). Creedon was the first to enter the ring. He weighed 158 pounds, while Fitzsimmons tipped the beam at 155½. The seconds for Creedon were Thomas Tracey, Mike Dunn, Tommy White and Charley Daly. Fitzsimmons was looked after by Jack Dempsey, James Dwyer, Kid McCoy and Samuel H. Stern.

The fight was of short duration. In the second round, when the two men had boxed each other four minutes, three heavy lefts, delivered in rapid succession on Creedon's nose, knocked the latter out.

DAN CREEDON,

Australia.

JACK DEMPSEY,

"THE NONPAREIL."

ACK DEMPSEY, who again lays claim to the title, "Middle-Weight Champion of the World," the acknowledged "Nonpareil" of pugilists, who in a career in the squared circle dating back to 1883, has fought fifty-one battles, six of which were draws and two defeats, was born at Curran, County Kildare, Ireland, December 15, 1862. He went to America with his parents when but a mere lad. The family settled in Brooklyn, New York, and Jack attended the public schools. When quite a lad he acquired great proficiency as a wrestler, and won many matches in New York, Boston and elsewhere.

In 1883 he decided to enter the prize ring, and at the age of twenty years, with a weight of 128 pounds, he met Edward McDonald, of Brooklyn, who stood five feet, seven and one-half inches and weighed 130 pounds, at a well-known training resort on the North River, New York City, April 7, 1883, for a purse of $100 (£20). The battle lasted twenty-seven rounds, occupying thirty-six minutes, and Dempsey was declared the winner. From this time on the pugilistic star of the "Nonpareil" was in the ascendant, and to more than briefly catalogue some of his prominent battles would be impossible in the limits of this article.

Among those he has met and defeated were the following:—George Fulljames, $1,000 (£200) a side, near New York City, July 30, 1884, in twenty-two rounds, lasting thirty-nine minutes; Tom Henry, for a purse of $1,000 (£200), in New York City, in six rounds, lasting twenty-three minutes; Billy Frazier, for a purse of $500 (£100), in the Alhambra, New York City, November 20, 1884, in five rounds, lasting eighteen minutes; Charley Bixamos, for a purse of $1,000 (£200), at Sportsman's Park, New Orleans, La., March 19, 1885, in five rounds, lasting eighteen minutes; Jack Keenan, for a purse of $1,000 (£200), at Golden Gate Park, San Francisco, California, July 20, 1885, in two rounds, lasting eleven minutes; Dave Campbell, for a purse of $1,000 (£200), at Portland, Oregon, November 2, 1885, in three rounds, lasting ten minutes and thirty seconds; Jack Fogarty, for a purse of $3,000 (£600), near New York City, February 2, 1886, in twenty-seven rounds, lasting one hour and fifty-one minutes; Peter McCoy, for a purse of $1,000 (£200), at Jersey City, New Jersey, February 24, 1886, in six rounds, lasting twenty-three minutes; George La Blanche, "The Marine," for a purse of $3,500, and the middle weight championship of the world, at Larshmont, L. I., March 14, 1886, in three rounds, lasting fifty minutes; Johnny Reagan, for a purse of $2,000 (£400) near New York City, in two rings, December 13, 1887, in forty-five rounds, lasting one hour and nine minutes; Dominick McCaffrey, for the gate receipts, at Pavonia Rink, Jersey City, New Jersey, January 31, 1888, in ten rounds, lasting thirty-nine minutes; Billy McCarthy, for a purse of $1,800 (£360), at San Francisco, California, February 18, 1890, in twenty-eight rounds, lasting one hour and fifty-two minutes.

On August 27, 1889, Dempsey was defeated by George La Blanche, "The Marine," at San Francisco, California, for a purse of $2,500 (£500) in thirty-two rounds, lasting two hours and seven minutes, and on January 14, 1891, at New Orleans, La., for a purse of $12,000 (£2,400) and the middle-weight championship of America, by Bob Fitzsimmons, in thirteen rounds, lasting forty-nine minutes.

JACK DEMPSEY,

"The Nonpareil."

PROF. MIKE DONOVAN,

INSTRUCTOR OF BOXING, NEW YORK ATHLETIC CLUB.

ICHAEL J DONOVAN was born in Chicago, Illinois, of Irish parents, in 1858. His first sight of a prize ring was at St. Louis, in July, 1866, when he stepped into one to fight Billy Cromley with bare knuckles, a contest of ninety-two rounds, lasting three hours and fifteen minutes, losing on a foul. He knew very little about boxing at this time, but acquired proficiency in the art, and meeting Mike Conroy, at St. Louis, defeated him in sixty-two rounds, lasting two hours and nine minutes.

His subsequent battles may be summarized as follows: Beat Jim Conroy, 175 pounds, at Memphis, Tennessee, 1866; conquered Patsy Curtin in five rounds, same year, at St. Louis; in 1867 beat Pat McDermott, 185 pounds, in four rounds, at Chicago; same year beat Dan Carr, 160 pounds, in one round, at Grand Haven, Michigan; in 1868 beat Pat Kelly, 175 pounds, in seven rounds, lasting fourteen minutes; near Indianapolis, Indiana, in January, 1869, he defeated John Boyne, in twenty-three rounds, lasting thirty-three minutes.

At this time $500 (£100) was considered a large purse to fight for, and growing weary of the small profit in ring contests, Donovan went back to his trade of ship-caulker after his fight with Boyne, and worked at it steadily until 1872, when he went to New York and resumed pugilism, at Harry Hill's, on Houston street. In the spring of 1872 he beat Jack Curtin in two rounds, a man named Jordan in three rounds, and Teddy Neary in three rounds. Subsequently he met and defeated Jack Lawrence in two rounds, and Byron McNeill in three rounds.

In 1873, at Philadelphia, he fought Jim Murray a draw in forty-five rounds, lasting one hour and five minutes, and in 1874, at the same place, he boxed four rounds with Charley Burke. At Troy, N. Y., in 1877, he beat Dick Liston, in five rounds, and in April, 1878, lost on a foul to W. C. McClellan, in fourteen rounds, lasting fifty-five minutes, for the middle-weight championship of America. In May, of the same year, he beat McClellan in seven rounds, lasting seventeen minutes; in August, 1878, at Virginia City, Nevada, he stopped Billy Costello in two rounds: at San Francisco beat George Crockett, in two rounds; fought a ninety-six round draw with W. C. McClellan, lasting three hours and forty-eight minutes, and at Sacramento, California, stopped George Smith in three rounds.

In February, 1880, he fought four hard rounds with John L. Sullivan, at Boston, Mass., and in October of the same year fought Ed. McGlensky a draw in five rounds; subsequently defeating him in three rounds. On March 22, 1881, he met John L. Sullivan the second time at Music Hall, Boston, fighting four rounds; in the same month, at Terrace Garden, New York, he met George Rourke, the police interfering in the third round, and in the fall of the same year met Rourke for the second time, the latter walking off the stage at the end of the third round.

In August, 1882, at the American Institute, New York, he boxed a three round draw with Jack Davis, of England, and in October, 1884, after teaching boxing for two years he beat Jack Welsh, at Philadelphia, in four rounds. In the same month he defeated Walter Watson, in New York, in seven rounds. After this battle he became boxing instructor at the New York Athletic Club, which position he has held ever since.

PROF. MIKE DONOVAN,

New York Athletic Club.

JACK FOGARTY.

PHILADELPHIA.

JACK FOGARTY, who gave Jack Dempsey the fight of his life, was born in the Third Ward, Philadelphia, December 24, 1865. As a lad he was pretty handy with his fists, and boxing came to him by intuition. His first public appearance as a boxer was as one of the competitors in John H. Clarke's middle-weight tournament in 1885. Jack was anxious to see the boxing, but he had no money to pay for an admission ticket, and without seriously intending it, entered himself in the tournament that he might secure free admission to the show. Much to his surprise he defeated every man put against him, and won the prize that was offered.

Jim McGrannigan he put out in two rounds; Denny McLaughlin, of Port Richmond, he silenced in three rounds; fought a draw with Frank Siffel, and at the second meeting defeated him in four rounds, and had the same experience with Jack Cook. At this time Fogarty was working in a large establishment as a packer and shipper; but he frequented the sporting resorts in the Quaker City at night, and in 1885–6 defeated Fred. Woods in two rounds, and knocked out Bill Gabig, "The Mysterious Boxer," in one round. A score of lesser lights who boxed him did so to their sorrow, and in the spring of 1886 he took a trip to Troy, N. Y., where he defeated Hughes, "The Dangerous Blacksmith," in two rounds, and Con. Tobin, who stood six feet two inches in height, and weighed 210 pounds, he knocked out in two rounds.

A match was made for him with "Hartford Dave," and the two men met with bare knuckles on Pleasure Island, which is in the Hudson River between Troy and Albany. Fogarty won an easy victory over his burly antagonist in five rounds. Subsequently in Pittsburg, Pa., he defeated Billson Jack in three rounds, and Ed. Delahanty in one round. Oweney McCann, of Philadelphia, also fell a victim to his skill and strength at Jimmy Ryan's old place, Fourth and Oxford Streets, being knocked out in four rounds.

In the early part of 1886, Fogarty was matched to fight Jack Kelly, of Port Richmond, but the negotiations fell through, and a match was arranged with Jack Dempsey instead. It was for $2,500 (£500) a side, and a purse of $1,000 (£200) and came off February 2, 1886, in New York City. Fogarty took but ten days in which to prepare for the battle. He was seconded by Arthur Chambers, and the Editor of "Pugilists of America and their Contemporaries." Dempsey was looked after by Gus Tuthill, his manager, and Tom Cleary, of California, his trainer. Al. Smith was referee. Dempsey weighed 143½ pounds, while Fogarty tipped the beam at 140½ pounds. Twenty-seven desperate rounds, lasting one hour and fifty-one minutes, were fought, Fogarty being terribly punished.

The Philadelphia boy was game to the last, and Dempsey had so much respect for his courage and ability to take and receive punishment, that he would never meet him again, although Fogarty tried to arrange another match afterwards. Failing in this he challenged George La Blanche, "The Marine." Nothing ever came of it, however, and Fogarty retired from the ring and devoted himself to politics, and the handling and training of pugilists. He was constable for six years in the Third Ward, Philadelphia, and his term expiring in April, 1894, he was urged to stand for the Legislature, but declined, because of private business. He lives in Philadelphia, was for several years manager of the Ariel Athletic Club; is married, and very domestic in his habits.

JACK FOGARTY,

Philadelphia.

JIM HALL.

AUSTRALIA.

IM HALL was born in Sydney, Australia, July 22, 1868. He is a pleasant-faced young man, and there is nothing in his appearance suggesting the fighter. He is six feet, one-half inch tall, and weighs, when in condition, about 160 pounds. He is a plasterer by trade and took up boxing for fun, his teacher being Billy McCarthy.

On March 10, 1889, he made his initial appearance as a pugilist, meeting George White, under London Prize Ring rules, for $500 (£100) a side. He was declared the winner in seven rounds. He defeated "Starlight," champion middle weight of Australia, May 8, 1889, in twenty rounds, Marquis of Queensbury rules, for a purse of $1,000 (£200). On July 10th, of the same year, he again met "Starlight," for a purse of $1,500 (£300), and defeated him in five rounds.

Ten days later, July 20th, he fought Jack Molloy, under Queensbury rules, for a purse of $1,000 (£200), and won in six rounds. He supplemented this by knocking Jim Nolan out, for a purse of $1,500 (£300), in seven rounds. On September 4th, he failed to knock out Jim Burgess in ten rounds, at Sydney; but the next day he settled Jack Slavin in ten rounds, Marquis of Queensbury rules, for a purse of $2,500 (£500). His eighth battle was with Jim Dolan, the heavy weight champion, for a purse of $1,500 (£300), October 20th, Hall winning in the fifth round. On November 3d, he defeated Herbert Goddard, for a purse of $1,500 (£300), in three rounds. Three weeks later, he again met Goddard for a similar purse, and defeated him in the same number of rounds.

On December 5, 1889, he defeated Eddie Welsh, in five rounds, for a purse of $1,500 (£300). Early in 1890 he fought a draw of fifteen rounds with James Fogarty, for a purse of $800 (£160). He then defeated Peter Boland for a purse of $2,500 (£500), in ten rounds, and later defeated the same man in eight rounds. His fifteenth battle was with Pablo Fanque, for a purse of $500 (£100), which he won with ease, in four rounds. He settled "Tutt" Ryan in five rounds, for a purse of $1,000 (£200), and later claimed to have knocked out Bob Fitzsimmons, in three and one-half rounds, for a purse and the gate receipts. Fitzsimmons says, however, that he "threw" the fight for a consideration of $75 (£15). He defeated "Dummy Mace" in five rounds; was beaten by Owen Sullivan in eleven rounds; and his old teacher, Billy McCarthy, bested him in eight rounds.

He went to America in 1892, landing in San Francisco, and was taken up by the California Athletic Club. Bested Alex. Greggains, subsequently defeating Bob Ferguson, champion heavy weight of Illinois, in three and a half rounds, for a purse of $3,000 (£600). He defeated Ted Pritchard in four rounds at Brighton, England, August 20, 1892, for $10,000 (£2,000), and on March 8, 1893, was defeated in four rounds, lasting thirteen minutes, by Bob Fitzsimmons, at New Orleans, La., for a purse of $40,000 (£8,000). Hall's last fight was with Paddy Slavin, at London, England, May 29, 1893, for a purse of $13,500 (£2,700), he winning in seven rounds, lasting twenty-seven minutes.

JIM HALL,
Australia.

TED PRITCHARD.

ENGLAND.

ED PRITCHARD, England's premier middle weight, is a Londoner. He was born in a suburb of that city, in 1866, and has resided there all his life. He could never be induced to visit America, although at one time the Crescent City Athletic Club, of New Orleans, offered him a match with the then undefeated Californian middle weight, Alexander Greggains, for a $6000 (£1,200) purse. He preferred to stay at home to meet Frank P. Slavin, for a small purse and $1,500 (£300) a side. This match, however, fell through.

Pritchard's most notable fight was with Jem Smith, the ex-champion heavy weight of England, whom he disposed of in a very short battle. In this fight, however, he did not gain the title of heavy weight champion, for that title was held by Peter Jackson.

The next most notable battle was with Jack Burke, the "Irish Lad," who succumbed to the prowess of Pritchard in short order. Burke had previously fought a draw with Charlie Mitchell.

The only defeat recorded against Pritchard was administered by Jim Hall, the celebrated Australian, who gained a victory over the English fighter in four rounds, August 20, 1892, at Brighton, England.

Pritchard has a style peculiarly his own. He stands well forward with his left arm extended to its full limit, and depends largely on his right to do the effective work. He fights at the middle weight limit, 154 pounds.

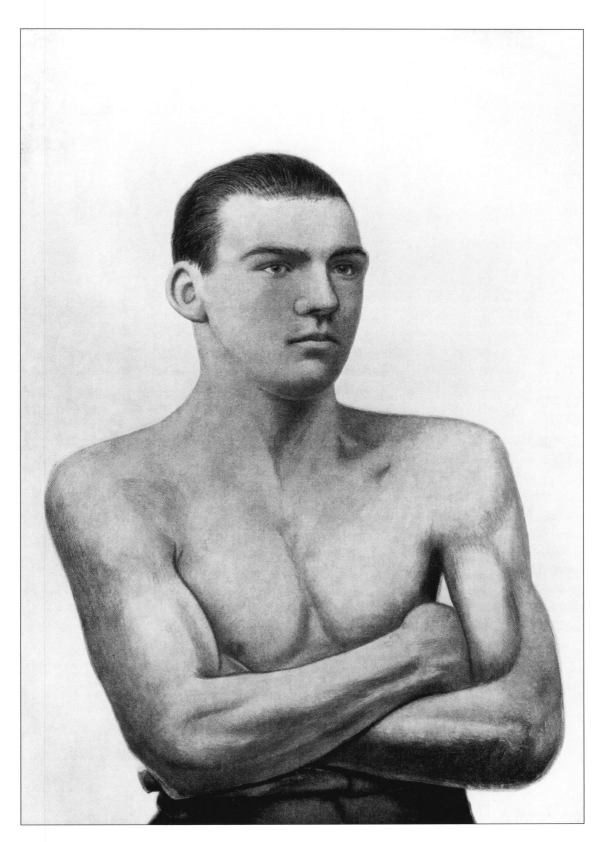

TED PRITCHARD,

England.

STEVE O'DONNELL,

CHAMPION CORBETT'S SPARRING PARTNER.

STEVE O'DONNELL, who is at present the boxing partner of James J. Corbett, champion of the world, was born at Williams River, Sydney, New South Wales, April 20, 1866. His mother was born in Kilkenny, and his father in Cork, Ireland. He stands six feet in height, and weighs 190 pounds.

He claims the title of champion heavy weight pugilist of Australia, through the outcome of four fistic engagements. His first battle was fought at 154 pounds for the amateur middle weight championship of Australia, with George Seal, and resulted in a draw after four rounds had been fought.

After this battle he entered the professional arena, and meeting Mike Dooley, defeated the latter in six rounds. He then retired from ring contests and started a boxing school. In 1892 he contracted to knock out Dick Burker in eight rounds, but did it in two. He afterwards defeated Chris Smithers, better known as "Black Chris," the colored champion of Queensland. O'Donnell had to stop him in eight rounds, and he knocked him out in three.

His last fight in Australia was with Ned Ryan, for $1,000 (£200) a side, the gate money, and heavy weight championship of Australia. The fight was decided in the California Athletic Club, Sydney, New South Wales, on February 14, 1893. The contest was to be the best of twenty rounds, but the police stopped it in the tenth round. O'Donnell agreed to finish the fight, but Ryan refused The former left the ring without a mark.

O'Donnell went to America in the spring of 1893, and after defeating John L. Cattanach, of Providence, Rhode Island, heavy weight champion of New England, at Coney Island, met George Godfrey, with whom he fought a six-round draw. Upon the return of Champion Corbett from Europe, in the fall of 1894, O'Donnell became his sparring partner, and Corbett wanted to back the Australian to a finish fight with Bob Fitzsimmons; but "Fitz" was after larger game, and finally arranged a match with Corbett himself.

STEVE O'DONNELL,

Australia.

Champion Corbett's Present Sparring Partner.

JACK McAULIFFE,

CHAMPION LIGHT WEIGHT OF THE WORLD.

JACK McAULIFFE, the Light Weight Champion of the World, was born in Cork, Ireland, March 24, 1866. He was yet very young when his parents emigrated to America, and settled at Bangor, Me. He was apprenticed to a cooper in Brooklyn (Williamsburgh), N. Y., as soon as he was able to work. Here he was a shop-mate of the famous ex-nonpareil Jack Dempsey.

McAuliffe's first appearance in the ring was July 1, 1884, in New York, when he defeated a man known as Young Mace. His next opponents were: Mike Leary, July 3d; Patsey Hogan, W. Whitner, and J. Karcher, October 10th, all of whom he whipped. These contests brought confidence to him, and he went into the light weight amateur championship contests, March 28, 1885, which he won, defeating J. Ellingsworth, J. Sperry, and W. Ellingsworth. Ed. Wagner was his next victim, in two rounds. Then he won Billy Madden's tournament. Then, on May 12th, he won a tournament promoted by Billy Madden. His next victim was Billy Young, of Washington, November 15th. His next, in the order named: Buck McKenna, December 8th; Jack Hopper, twice, January 13 and February 27, 1886; Ed. Carroll; Charles (Bull) McCarthy, January 14, 1886. In 1886 he defeated Billy Frazier, in twenty rounds; then Harry Gilmore, in twenty-eight rounds. A four-round draw was the result of a second meeting with Gilmore, March 2d, and the same result was attained in a bout with Jimmy Mitchell, of Philadelphia, shortly afterwards.

On November 16, 1887, McAuliffe and Jem Carney, the English boxer, met and fought seventy-four rounds to a draw. On October 27, 1888, Patsy Kerrigan, John L. Sullivan's *protege*, and McAuliffe fought an even battle of ten rounds. On October 10, 1888, he knocked out Billy Dacey in eleven rounds. This was for the championship. Then he fought a four-round draw with Mike Daly. On December 17th he beat Sam Collyer, in two rounds: Jack Hyams was next worsted in nine rounds. On February 13, 1889, McAuliffe and Billy Myer fought sixty-four rounds to a draw. Mike Daly and McAuliffe met again on December 6, 1889, and fought fifteen rounds to a draw. March 2, 1890, McAuliffe and Jimmy Carroll met in San Francisco, and McAuliffe won in forty-seven rounds, after a most stubborn conflict.

It only took him three rounds to dispose of Harry Gilmore before the Manhattan Athletic Club in New York. He won from Austin Gibbons at the Granite Athletic Club in Hoboken, September 1, 1891. Jere Dunn was the Referee, and his decision did not meet with favor, inasmuch, as the articles of agreement called for a finish fight, and Gibbons was not knocked out when the police interfered in the sixth round. On September 5th, 1892, he beat Billy Meyer in fifteen rounds before the Olympic Athletic Club in New Orleans. Then on April 1, 1893, he fought four rounds with Horace Leeds, at the Academy of Music, Philadelphia. When he met young Griffo at the Seaside Athletic Club, August 27, 1894, he had decidedly the worst of a ten-round bout; he, however, got the decision from the Referee. McAuliffe's most sensational fight was with Jim Carney, November 16, 1887, for the light weight championship of the world, which the mob broke up and the Referee declared a draw.

McAuliffe fights at the light weight limit, one hundred and thirty-three pounds.

JACK McAULIFFE,
Champion Light Weight of the World.

"YOUNG GRIFFO" (ALBERT GRIFFETHS),

CHAMPION FEATHER WEIGHT OF AUSTRALIA.

YOUNG GRIFFO, of Australia, is probably the most remarkable pugilist yet sent to America by the Antipodes. He went to fight George Dixon, the dusky champion, and in a twenty-round bout, in Boston, on June 29, 1894, the decision was a draw. It has been asserted that Griffo was not trying his utmost in this bout with the hope of getting on a finish battle.

Griffo was born "on the rocks," at Miller's Point, Sydney, New South Wales, Australia, in 1871, of very humble parentage. At the age of ten years he started in life on his own hook, selling papers on the streets of Sydney, and making a living the best way he could. The first indication of his pugnacity and ability was shown, when a boy named Scott tried to bully him, and whom he polished off easily with natural science. This turned his bent towards pugilism, and he secured a match with Bob Quigley, whom he defeated in fifteen rounds.

He then secured an engagement at Foley's Hall, the star boxing place of Sydney, and launched himself fairly on the sea of pugilism, meeting all comers with unvarying success, although often conceding a handicap of many pounds. Pluto, a dusky boxer, of Melbourne, gave Griffo considerable trouble. They met five times, and the results were draws of eight, six, twenty-three, thirteen, and seventy rounds respectively.

Australian Billy Murphy, who was then in the first flight of feather weights, undertook to stop Griffo in four rounds, but failed. Although weighing but 112 pounds, Griffo won Sam Matthews' 140-pound competition. Young O'Brien, of Queensland, undertook to stop him in eight rounds, but was nearly stopped himself. A twenty-round draw was the result of a meeting with Abe Willis, but later Griffo stopped him in three rounds.

Nipper Peaks was counted the cleverest 126-pounder in Australia, but Griffo out-pointed him, and won easily. George McKenzie then undertook to stop Griffo in fifteen rounds, but signally failed.

On June 12, 1890, Young McLeod tried to put Griffo out in fifteen rounds, but was knocked out himself in two rounds. Griffo obtained his first world-wide reputation when he met Billy Murphy at the Sydney Athletic Club, September 13th, 1890, and in the sixteenth round Murphy pulled off the gloves and would not continue, claiming that the gloves had been tampered with. Murphy afterwards admitted that Griffo had him beaten. Griffo beat Murphy again June 22, 1893, when the fight was awarded to him in the twenty-second round. Griffo and Jem Barron boxed a twenty-two round draw in Sydney, July 25, 1892, and at the same place, on November 8, he put a twenty-five round draw with Martin Denny to his credit. He was awarded the decision twice over Jerry Marshall, the first time in Sydney, December 20, 1892, when the police interfered, and later when the ring was rushed and Marshall accused of committing a foul.

Since his advent in America Griffo has proved that the stories of his wonderful prowess in Australia were not exaggerated. On January 3, 1894, he met Solly Smith in Chicago—in a bout of six rounds, and although Griffo had all the better of matters the decision was a draw. Twenty days later he met Johnny Van Herst, in a conditional contest, and it ended like the one with Smith. Neither man hit him once. In an eight-round contest between Griffo and George Lavigne in Chicago, February 10, 1894, the battle was very even throughout, and a draw was declared.

"YOUNG GRIFFO" AND WALTER CAMPBELL
"IN POSITION."

OWEN H. ZIEGLER,

PHILADELPHIA.

WEN H. ZIEGLER is a Philadelphian, having been born in Lansdale, a suburb of Philadelphia, January 4, 1871. He comes of Quaker stock and never showed more than ordinary pugnacity until he entered into some sparring competitions, held by the First Regiment, N. G. of Pa., of which he was a member when he secured a four-round draw with Gilbert Roomer, a very clever amateur.

His work on that occasion attracted considerable attention, and he was induced to join the Athletic Club of the Schuylkill Navy, Philadelphia, and under its colors won the light weight amateur championship, December 17 and 19, 1891, when he defeated Charles Hendrickson, Joe Harmon, "Chuck" Conners, and John Hannegan. His first professional contest was with Jimmy Fox, of Philadelphia, over whom he got the decision in four rounds. Denny Butler was the Referee.

Ziegler's hardest fight was with Horace M. Leeds. They met at Atlantic City, August 20, 1894, and fought four fiercely contested rounds. There was no decision given. H. Walter Schlichter, of Philadelphia, was the Referee, and the opinion as to the victor in the bout was very evenly divided.

Ziegler has gained decisions over the following men : John Anderson in one round; Arthur Woods in one round; John Boomerstein in one round; Gus Fulmer in four rounds; Jerome Quigley in three rounds; Pat Sheehan, of Bethlehem, in three rounds; Bob Lewis in one round; Arthur Kelly in one round; Gus Gross, at Malvern, in two rounds; Frank Fisher, Conshohocken, in three rounds; Joe Kirm, Conshohocken, in three rounds; Charles Kirm in three rounds; J. S Harmon, Philadelphia, in three rounds; Jimmy Hagen in four rounds; Billy McLaughlin in four rounds; Joe Einstein, at Shenandoah, Pa., in seventeen rounds; Joe Gitt, a middle weight, at Hanover, Pa., in twenty-seven rounds, and again in eleven rounds; Billy Arnold, at Reading, Pa., in three rounds; Wayne Kline, at Reading, Pa., in four rounds; Joe Harmon again, in three rounds; Billy Peterson in four rounds; Al O'Brien in two rounds; "Beitch" Wilkinson, of Ohio, (a heavy weight) in thirty-seven rounds; Frank Bowen, of Ohio, in seven rounds; George Reynolds in six rounds; Jimmy McHale in two rounds; Eddie Ryan, New York, in six rounds; Wayne Kline in two rounds; Peter Murray, of Trenton, in four rounds; Jimmy Mullen in four rounds; Al O'Brien in three rounds; Charles (Bull) McCarthy in six rounds; Charles McKeever, of Norristown, in four rounds; W. McManus, of Brooklyn, in one round, and Billy Ernest, of Brooklyn, in six rounds.

Ziegler and Stanton Abbott met in August, 1893, in Philadelphia, and sparred four rounds to a draw, but when they met again on October 13, 1894, Ziegler had decidedly the better of the bout. Ziegler stands five feet eight inches in height, and fights best at one hundred and thirty pounds. He generally weighs about one hundred and forty pounds.

OWEN H. ZIEGLER,

Philadelphia, Pa.

JIMMY CARNEY,

LIGHT WEIGHT CHAMPION OF ENGLAND.

AMES CARNEY was born of Irish parents in Birmingham, England, in 1857. He stands five feet four and one-half inches high, and his best fighting weight was one hundred and thirty-three pounds. Carney took to pugilism in 1878, when he was pitted against Paddy Giblin for $50 (£10), and won in eleven minutes, breaking Giblin's jaw. On April 9, 1879, near Birmingham, he met Paddy Lee for $50 (£10) a side. Carney won after a severe battle lasting two hours. He next beat Pat Downey, of London, for $250 (£50) in thirty-five minutes, near London. On July 21, 1880, he fought "Punch" Callon for $500 (£100). The ground was sloppy and it rained during the greater part of the battle. Seventy-four rounds were fought in two hours and two minutes, when both men were nearly helpless, and a draw was declared.

Carney with Sam Breeze, Charles Hopkin and Jim Walder, visited the United States in April, 1881, and for some weeks boxed at Owney Geoghegan's, on the Bowery, New York City. During the engagement there Carney disposed of Sam Breeze in five rounds, in a big glove fight for a purse. In the fall of the same year he returned home, and signed articles to fight Jimmy Highland at one hundred and twenty-eight pounds for $125 (£25) a side. They met near Farnsworth, October 11, 1881, and after a desperate battle of forty-three rounds, occupying an hour and forty-five minutes, the police appeared and broke up the mill; a draw was declared. Highland's ribs were broken and he was so badly punished about the face and body, that he died four days afterwards. Carney was arrested and tried for manslaughter. It was proved that Highland's injuries resulted from improper care of himself, but Carney was convicted of prize fighting, and on February 15, 1882, was sentenced to six months imprisonment.

Carney's last engagement in English prize fighting was near London, on December 20, 1884, when he met Jack Hyams for $2500 (£500) and the light weight championship of Great Britain. Carney won in forty-five rounds, lasting one hour and forty-five minutes.

Carney and Jack McAuliffe met at Revere Beach, near Boston, Mass., on Wednesday, November 16, 1889, and contested seventy-four desperate rounds, when McAuliffe's friends broke into the ring, and the fight was declared postponed, and eventually a draw. Carney weighed one hundred and twenty-nine pounds, and McAuliffe one hundred and thirty-one pounds, and the former had the better of the battle all through.

JIMMY CARNEY,
Light Weight Champion of England.

GEORGE LA BLANCHE,

"THE MARINE."

EORGE LA BLANCHE, better known as "The Marine," was born of French parents at South Quebec, Point Levi, Canada, December 19, 1856. His proper name is George Blais. He stands five feet six inches in height, and weighs in condition one hundred and fifty pounds. He first took to boxing in 1882, when a driver in Battery "B," Canadian Light Artillery. At that time he fought J. Putnam at the Quebec Citadel. Putnam's weight was one hundred and ninety pounds, but "The Marine" whipped him in four rounds, breaking his left hand in doing it.

On December 11, 1883, he joined the Marine service at Boston, but through the influence of a number of prominent sporting men he secured his discharge, and on January 28, 1884, he fought George Smith, a heavy weight, a six-round draw at the Cribb Club. March 21, 1884, he whipped Tom Bates, of England, in five rounds. His next victim was Denny Kelleher, who succumbed in four rounds. This was on October 3d, at the Cribb Club. Pete McCoy, then champion middle weight, was induced to meet him in April, 1885, at the Boston Boxing Club, in an eight-round fight, which was declared a draw.

La Blanche's performance with McCoy so elated his admirers that he was matched with Jack Dempsey. They fought Sunday, March 14, 1886, at Larshmont, L. I., for $2,000 (£400), and a $500 (£100) purse. "The Marine" was defeated in thirteen rounds, lasting forty-nine minutes and five seconds.

His next battles were as follows: Defeated Mike Gillespie, in four rounds, at Hoboken, N. J., October 24, 1887; beat Harry Langdon in three rounds, October 26, same place; beat Bill Dunn in three rounds, same place; drew with Jack Fallon in six rounds, December 22, 1887; beat Jack Varley in thirteen rounds, near Yonkers, N. Y., August 18, 1888. His greatest battle was with Jack Dempsey "The Nonpareil," whom he knocked out in thirty-two rounds, at the California Athletic Club, with the pivot blow, which was made famous by this fight. This was Dempsey's first defeat. The battle took place August 27th, for a purse of $5,500 (£1,100).

He was defeated by George Kessler in thirteen rounds at Butte, Montana, November 3, 1890. Since then he has done but little fighting.

GEORGE LA BLANCHE,
"The Marine."

AUSTIN GIBBONS.

PATERSON, N. J.

USTIN GIBBONS is a Jerseyman. He was born in 1870, and was even in early youth athletically inclined. His first professional battle was with Luke Clark from whom he won in six rounds. He next disposed of George Young in three rounds, then George Butler in eleven rounds, Joe Siddy in five, Frank Moon in nine, and Jack Kenny in seven. On December 14, 1889, Mike Cushing lost in twenty-four rounds. On November 7, 1890, Gibbons and Cushing met again, and Gibbons again won; this time in nineteen rounds. Gibbons was then promised a match in San Francisco, but was fooled. He went to New Orleans after Andy Bowen; but that gentleman refused to sign articles. He went to London where he got on a match with Jim Verrall, a prominent English light weight, whom he whipped in four rounds. His next battle was with Jack McAuliffe the light weight champion. They met at the Granite Athletic Club, Hoboken, N. J., September 1, 1891, and, after fighting six terrific rounds, McAuliffe was declared the winner, although Gibbons was not done by any means. The Referee was Jere Dunn, and a great many fair-minded sports thought the decision a most unjust one. A draw would have been the right verdict. Gibbons' next battle also resulted disastrously to him. He was matched to do battle for ten rounds with Joe Walcott, a sturdy black, and had to succumb to his terrific blows in four rounds. This took place at Coney Island, before the American Athletic Club on October 15, 1894, and was for a good-sized purse. Gibbons' best fighting weight was one hundred and thirty-three pounds, and it was at that figure that he made nearly all his matches.

AUSTIN GIBBONS,

Paterson, N. J.

PROF. JOHN H. CLARK,

PHILADELPHIA, PA.

JOHN H. CLARK is a native of Erin's Green Isle, having been born in County Galway, May 18, 1849. He arrived in America just after he had attained his majority, the exact date being June 11, 1870. He stands five feet six and one-half inches in his stocking feet, and ordinarily weighs about one hundred and forty-five pounds. In his early youth he had mastered the intricacies of clog and jig dancing, and he began public life by giving exhibitions of his really wonderful skill in that line. These exhibitions brought him in contact with sparrers, and he at once developed an aptitude and a liking for that sport. His first appearance was at "The Arbor," 40 West Houston Street, New York City. On November 30, 1871, he engaged in a three-round glove contest with Arthur Chambers; but he was inexperienced, and Chambers got the decision. Shortly after this, Clark went to Philadelphia, where he opened a sparring and dancing school in conjunction with Jim Colbert and Bill Faldon, on Arch Street, near Second.

He had improved greatly in his sparring, developing into a very fine boxer, and had several very sensational settoes, with the then light weight champion, Billy Edwards, on the stage of Mortimer's Varieties, and the Grand Central Theatre, Philadelphia. The feeling engendered by these contests led to Clark, on August 26, 1876, issuing a challenge backed with $50 (£10) to Edwards, to fight for the light weight championship and $2500 (£500) a side. To this Edwards replied that he had retired from the ring forever, thus leaving the championship an open question.

In 1878, Clark opened a billiard room and boxing school at 1117 Filbert Street which he conducted for some years. His greatest battle was the one for the light weight championship with Arthur Chambers, which took place March 27, 1879, at Long Point, Canada. The battle was fought under London Prize Ring Rules, and lasted two hours and twenty minutes, one hundred and thirty-six rounds being contested. Clark in this fight showed that he was a thoroughly game pugilist, but that he had been trained too fine. The fight was stopped when Clark was literally held down in his chair. Clark claims to this day that the scales were fixed, and that Chambers was over weight. This battle was fought on a Thursday, and on the following Monday the men met again at the Grand Central Theatre, Philadelphia, and the fight was so hot that the curtain was rung down in the second round; during which Clark had all the better of the contest. A second match was partially arranged, but it fell through.

After this, Clark opened the Olympic Club, on the corner of Eighth and Vine Streets, Philadelphia; where for four years he conducted glove contests, at which all the prominent pugilists of the world appeared. During Mayor Fitler's administration Clark made a tour of the West with a variety combination, offering $50 (£10) to any one within ten pounds of his weight, whom he could not best in four rounds. Although the best boxers all through the Western States tried for it, not one got the $50 (£10).

Clark is forty-six years of age, but is still willing to meet any light weight in the world in a four round contest for scientific points. He is now proprietor of the American Athletic Club in Philadelphia.

PROF. JOHN H. CLARK,

Philadelphia, Pa.

JIMMY CARROLL.

ENGLAND.

JIMMY CARROLL—whose right name, by the way, is James Fleming—is an Englishman by birth. He was born in Lambeth, London, England, in 1852. He has fought a number of bare-knuckle fights in England in which he was invariably victorious. His first battle in America was with Billy Frazier, on March 23, 1878, which was declared a draw. Since then he has been actively engaged in the ring, having defeated a number of good men, most prominent among whom are the following: Charley King, Puck Sullivan, James Casby, Ike Bamburg, M. T. Scully, William Sullivan, Ed. S. Bartlett, Tommy McManus, Sam Blakelock and Mike Lucie; he has fought draws with Patsy Kerrigan and Mike Daly. Carroll also fought McAuliffe for $13,000 (£2,600), and the light weight championship, but McAuliffe knocked him out in the forty-seventh round, after a very hard battle, lasting three hours and seven minutes. He then, on September 16, 1890, for a purse of $3,500 (£700) fought Andy Bowen, the New Orleans light weight, besting him in twenty-one rounds.

December 21, 1891, for a purse of $5,000 (£1000) at New Orleans, Myer reversed the decision, and won from Carroll in forty-five rounds, lasting two hours and forty-five minutes.

Carroll weighs one hundred and thirty-five pounds in condition, and stands five feet six inches in height.

JIMMY CARROLL,

England.

SAMUEL BLAKELOCK,

ENGLAND.

SAMMY BLAKELOCK, one of the best light weight pugilists and trainers, ever turned out by England, was born about 1864. He was very successful with his opponents in his native land, and after running the gauntlet there made up his mind to visit America in an effort to win the light weight championship. He, however, got no further than a match with Jimmy Carroll, for a $1500 (£300) purse which was hung up by the California Athletic Club, San Francisco, Cal. The match took place March 19, 1890, and after fifteen of the most desperate rounds ever seen in California Carroll was declared the winner. Blakelock weighed one hundred and thirty-one pounds, while Carroll scaled one pound heavier. Hiram Cook was the Referee.

Blakelock returned to England then, but returned to America as the trainer for Dick Burge who came to this country for a match with Jack McAuliffe, but which he was unable to make. Blakelock's best fighting weight was one hundred and twenty-eight pounds.

The London *Sporting Life* of November 7, 1894, printed the following: "This famous boxer and trainer is lying seriously ill at his residence in Battersea with bronchitis and inflammation of the lungs. Sam was engaged to train Dick Burge for his match with Ted Pritchard, and though this unfortunate indisposition will prevent him from fulfilling his contract with Burge, it is to be hoped he will soon be convalescent and in a position to second Dick on the eventful night"

SAMUEL BLAKELOCK,
Birmingham, England.

MIKE DALY

BANGOR, ME.

IKE DALY was born in Bangor, Me., in 1862. His first contest was with Martin Daly in 1883. It lasted seven rounds, and Mike Daly won. He defeated M. Baker in four rounds, October 15, 1884, at Bangor; Billy Chandler in three rounds, October, 1885, at Bangor; Ed. Kelsey in sixteen rounds, October 20, 1885, at Winfield, N. Y., with bare knuckles; J. Meehan in eight rounds, January 31, 1887, at Bangor, Me.; J. McDonald in three rounds, March 18, 1887, at Augusta, Me.; Walter Campbell in six rounds, May 17, 1887, at Boston; Billy Frazier in seven rounds, June 15, 1887, at Boston; Joe Donovan in two rounds, in February, 1890, at Rockland, Me.; Jim Dwyer in one round, May 27, 1890, at Lewiston, Me.; drew with Tom McManus in six rounds, October 12, 1885, at St. John's, N. B.; Jimmy Mitchell in six rounds, October 12, 1885; Jim Gibbons in six rounds; Jack McAuliffe in three rounds, January 16, 1886, in Boston, when the police stopped the fight; Jimmy F. Carroll in fifteen rounds, February 1, 1888, in Boston; Jack McAuliffe in fifteen rounds, December 5, 1889, at Boston.

The only defeat he has sustained was by Austin Gibbons, before whom he stayed for thirty-one rounds before succumbing. This fight took place March 7, 1894, at New Orleans.

Daly's fighting weight is one hundred and thirty-three pounds.